The Ultimate Boxer

Understanding the Sport and Skills of Boxing

Written by
Christy Halbert, Ph.D.

ISI Publishing, Brentwood, Tennessee

Library of Congress Cataloging-in-Publication Data
Halbert, Christy L. 1970–
The Ultimate Boxer: Understanding The Sport and Skills of Boxing
By Christy L. Halbert
p. cm.
Includes bibliographical references (p.) and index.
ISBN: 0-9630968-5-0 (pbk.)
1. Boxing—Training. 2. Exercise. 3. Physical education and training.
I. Title.

Library of Congress Control Number: 2003101614

ISBN: 0-9630968-5-0
Copyright 2003 by Christy L. Halbert

All rights reserved. Except for use in a review, the reproduction, transmission, or utilization of this work in any form or by any means, electronic or mechanical, now known or hereafter invented, including photocopying, xerography, recording, and in any information storage and retrieval system is forbidden without the written permission of the author. Cover design and Illustrations: Ernesto Lerma and Pepe Rodríguez; Additional illustrations: Christy Halbert; Common Foul and Referee Signal Illustrations courtesy of USA Boxing, Inc.; Chart found on page 192 courtesy of Canada Amateur Boxing Association; Printer: Vaughan Printing

Multiple copies of this book are available at a discount for sales promotions, premiums, fund-raising, or educational purposes. Direct requests for special editions or excerpts to ISI Publishing, a division of Impact Seminars, Inc.

Manufactured in the United States of America
10 9 8 7 6 5 4 3 2 1

ISI Publishing
A division of Impact Seminars, Inc.
P.O. Box 431
Brentwood, Tennessee 37024-0431
www.impactseminars.com

The author's informational website for this book can be found on the Internet at www.TheUltimateBoxer.com

An Important Message for Fitness and Competitive Boxers

Boxing is a contact sport. Participation in boxing implies acceptance of the risk of injury. Techniques outlined in this book are designed to help you box to your maximum potential; however, compliance with any of these techniques and safety instructions does not eliminate the risk of injury. Additionally, boxing safety equipment is designed to help minimize the chance and degree of injury, but will not prevent all injuries. You should consult a healthcare professional before participating in boxing or any other sport.

About the Illustrators

Ernesto Lerma and Pepe Rodríguez both earned degrees in Graphic Design and Advertising from the Centro de Estudios de las Américas in Merida, Mexico. They co-founded Swak in 2000.

Table of Contents

Preface 9
Acknowledgements 13

Chapter 1: Fundamentals and Skill Building

Sound Fundamentals 16
Think Feet 21
The Hands and Punching Reminders 25
The Jab and Duck 28
The Cross and Slip/Slide 32
The Hook, Parry/Catch, and Block 36
The Uppercuts and Half-Step Back 41
The Feint, Draw, and Side Step 44
Infighting, Covering, and Offensive Reminders 46
Making It All Come Together with Combinations 48

Chapter 2: Exercises and the Conditioning of the Boxer's Body

Practicing Technique Through Common Boxing Exercises . .52
Creating a Day's Workout 60
General Conditioning 62
Running Programs for Conditioning 68
Muscles Used for Boxing (Part I): Basic Stretches 72
Muscles Used for Boxing (Part II):
    Abdominal Muscles and Trunk Strength 77
Muscles Used for Boxing (Part III):
    Resistance Exercises that Improve Overall Strength 84
Increasing Your Power with Plyometric Training 95

Chapter 3: The Science of Boxing

Secrets to Success (Part I): Winning Bouts 108
Secrets to Success (Part II): Taking Advantage of Things
    Other Boxers Don't Do 111
Secrets to Success (Part III): Character Counts 113
Reading Your Opponent's Style 115
The Importance of Safety 117
Weight: Weight Loss and Making Weight 121
Techniques for Wrapping Hands 126
Boxer's Code of Conduct: Fouls, Infractions,
    and the Referee's Duty 130
Common Fouls and Referee Signals in Olympic-style Boxing .131

Chapter 4: Gaining the Strategic Advantage

The Rhythm of the Boxing Zone 136
Maximizing Your Defense 137
Defensive and Evasive Tactics 140
Angles, Angles, Angles 142
Variations on the Fundamentals 145
Punching with Power 148
Counterpunching and Counters for Counters 149
Punching to the Body 152
Putting Your Skills to the Test: Sparring 152
Working with a Novice Boxer in Sparring 158
Sparring with Boxers Who Are Better or Stronger Than You .161

Chapter 5: Keys to Successful Competition

Competition: Boxing Styles 164
Boxing a Shorter Opponent 165
Boxing a Taller Opponent 166
Boxing a Left-hander If You Are a Right-handed Boxer 167
Boxing a Wild Fighter 169
Boxing a Croucher 170
Boxing a Boxer 171
Boxing a Slugger 172

Boxing Specifically for Judges (Part I):
  Traditional & Computer Scoring Systems 174
Boxing Specifically for Judges (Part II):
  Judges' Positions at Ringside 179
Managing Ring Variables: Dimensions and
  Flooring Materials 183
What to Expect When You Box in Amateur Boxing Shows . .185
What to Expect If You Fight on Professional Cards 187

Chapter 6: Social Aspects of Boxing
The Difference Between Professional and Amateur Boxing 190
A Short History of Boxing 194
Race and Boxing 195
Women in Boxing 199
The Romance of Boxing 202
Medicine and Boxing Controversy: Head Trauma 203

Chapter 7: Coaching and Training Boxers
The Responsibility of the Coach 206
First Aid for Minor Injuries 207
Boxing Truths and Myths 208
Fitness Boxing 210

Chapter 8: Supportive Material
Offensive Arsenal Summary 212
Defensive Arsenal Summary 213
Defensive Strategies for Offensive Punches 214
Goals Worksheet 215
Combinations Worksheet 216
Self-Assessment of Boxing Skills 218
Getting Involved in the Sport 220
Informational Websites 221
Equipment and Apparel Resources 222
Movies About Boxing 223
Glossary of Boxing Terms 227
Bibliography 237
Index 239

Preface

I wrote this book because I believe that boxers should be educated in the theory and practice of their sport in order to reach their full potential in the ring. Educated boxers make better training choices, commit fewer fouls, box with confidence, understand why they won or lost a bout, and enjoy the process of learning to box. I hope the essays in this book will add to your enjoyment of the sport.

This book takes you beyond basic punches. *The Ultimate Boxer* is for all those interested in boxing principles, from amateur boxers to professionals, from fitness boxers to martial artists (especially those making a transition into boxing), from boxing coaches to boxing aficionados, to parents or partners of competitive boxers.

This book is not intended to replace the supervision, observation and guidance of a boxing coach. Use this handbook to complement your training, not replace a coach's instruction.

The Ultimate Boxer should be used as a handbook, giving you many resources to learn about all aspects of boxing. This information, coupled with hard work and effective training, will help you develop a boxing style of your own design. It is a compilation of information gathered from interviews with fellow coaches; from my experience teaching boxing certification courses for coaches and officials, as well as from my own experience as a boxer; from reading the research of social scientists and experts in physiology; and through coaching boxers who ask challenging questions about technique that usually go unquestioned (and unanswered) in gyms.

This book works best if you are boxing as you read it. It will improve your boxing, and as you practice what you learn here, you will better understand the principles set forth throughout the book.

The Ultimate Boxer encourages you to ask questions about your training. Ever wonder why you are supposed to keep your jab shoulder ahead of the other shoulder? Do you want to find out why you've been losing those close bouts you thought you had won? Need some new training ideas to keep yourself motivated? Ever wonder where that phrase, "the great white hope," originated? This book will answer these questions, and many more.

The nine chapters are comprised of short essays. Each essay is designed as a succinct summary of the principles of specific skills and strategies. Rather than asking you to practice skills a certain way, *The Ultimate Boxer* helps you understand proper technique and provides you with skill-building exercises to perfect your boxing form.

The beginning essays cover fundamentals of defense and offense, as well as training techniques and exercises to improve specific skills and overall performance. Later essays build on the fundamentals by taking your training and skills to an advanced level. Each essay contains points to remember when practicing a skill, exercises to sharpen skills, worksheet-style tables, questions to ask yourself, motivational slogans, or helpful lists. The last essays examine how boxing fits into our contemporary culture and explain some of the issues that have traditionally plagued the sport, such as racism, classism, and sexism. Taken together, these essays represent a complete examination of the sport of boxing, one that can help you become a better boxer.

The Spirit of Boxing

I've often been asked why I participate in the art of fighting. My answer is that boxing is not fighting: boxing is a sport. Boxers do not go into contests angry with each other. Inherent conflict is not present among boxers who compete against each other. Boxers, in fact, usually admire each other because they have a respect for each other, since boxing is an activity that involves mutual and voluntary participation. It is a sport based on skill and superb physical conditioning. Boxing is a laborious and challenging sport. Its practitioners know this fact well.

To be a good boxer you must practice like a good boxer. A good boxer is neither made overnight nor crowned after one big win. A good boxer is something you become. To be a good boxer, you must do what good boxers do: work hard to master the physical and mental aspects of the sport, commit to be in good physical condition, support your teammates, challenge your opponents, respect yourself and others, and play by the rules.

There is no such thing as a "natural boxer." No one is born with the knowledge of how to box. Everyone starts the same way, learning the same punches and defensive moves. Don't get frustrated when you don't think you are progressing fast enough. If you stick with it, you have the power to become a successful boxer.

The path to good boxing is training; this is the only way to succeed. You must learn to enjoy the process of good training. Training is necessary for both the body and the mind. A good boxer is curious and a hard worker, and wants every practice to be mentally and physically challenging. You must learn techniques and strategies, understand the theory behind them, and then be able to execute those skills in the ring. Further, you will not be able to execute your punches or strategy if you are not in good physical condition.

In boxing, you must train as though you will compete against someone better than you. You may face this eventuality every time you spar, or you may not face it in competition for years. The question is, what will you do once you meet this opponent? What if you win? What if you lose? What if you are overwhelmed? It is often said that what makes the difference is not how many times you are knocked down, but how many times you get up from knockdowns. A champion doesn't have to win every bout; in fact, few champions go without a loss in their career. A real champion is someone who can come back in a bout, someone who can come back after a defeat. A champion is someone who makes himself or herself stronger, faster and smarter in the face of a challenge. A champion is someone who gets back up and perseveres despite being tired or afraid.

All boxers have in common bravery and courage. Boxers step up and meet the challenge of the unknown—and all face fear when they step through the ropes. Courage is evident in those who win most of their bouts as well as in those who lose most of their bouts. The boxer who doesn't win his/her bout has still met fear and conquered it. The boxer who doesn't win this time may win the next bout. Boxing gives participants the ability to learn from mistakes, to distinguish between loss and gain, to figure out what we can do to make ourselves stronger.

Finally, a spirit of cooperation in amateur boxing brings together people from all types of backgrounds to participate in a demanding sport. There is an unwritten code of conduct among boxers that is thrilling to witness; it is the sense of respect that boxers hold for each other. Extraordinary camaraderie develops among individuals who box whether they are beginners or world champions. Coaches, officials, and other volunteers work with boxers to provide a safe and inclusive environment in which to participate in this ancient skill. To be a part of this environment, you need to be committed to being the best boxer possible: learn about boxing, develop your skills, learn from your mistakes, and get yourself in good physical condition.

> **Become your toughest opponent.**
> **Work hard.**

Acknowledgements

During the years I spent writing and developing this book, I benefited from the support of many friends and associates. I want to express my appreciation to those who helped make this book possible, realizing that countless people have influenced me throughout my years in boxing and athletics. Many individuals read, edited, and made suggestions to essay drafts. I found all of their comments helpful, including those by Angel Bovee and Kathy Kinnin. Special thanks are due to the expert readers: Evander Holyfield, Cappy Kotz, and Dr. Ken Cox.

Thanks also to all the open boxers, junior boxers, master's and fitness boxers who asked pertinent questions and made me evaluate every skill and drill that I incorporated into their training. Many thanks to countless boxing coaches from whom I learned things to do and not to do in my own coaching, who challenged me to find the link between theory and practice. Many coaches were generous in allowing me to coach along with them, especially George Ginter, TD Wortham, and Henry Vidal Gijón. Thanks go to the volunteer officials who took me under their wing to explain the intricacies of refereeing and judging: Marty Smith, Rosemarie and Richard Trindle, Linda De la Paz, Ken Butler, the late Pete Suazo, Jim Quigley, and Sandy Pino, among others. The continued support of Jeaneene and Dick Hildebrandt is always appreciated. Their enthusiasm for Olympic-style boxing has no match.

Sue Bryant and Scott Kale, from The Omni, readied the text and cover for publication. Dru, Tammy, and Tim, of Fields Publishing, offered advice and expertise related to the layout. Thanks also to my parents, John Halbert, who believed in this project enough to publish it, and Marjorie Halbert, who helped with editing. Ernesto Lerma and Pepe Rodríguez created numerous illustrations and showed patience while we experimented with the best ways to illustrate the skill concepts. Of course, my partner Chalene Helmuth deserves special mention as the first reader, editor, and source of constant support through the entire project.

Checklist for a Champion

☐ Do you look forward to going to the gym?

☐ Do you get to the gym early and stay as long as is needed?

☐ Do you work harder than anyone else in the gym?

☐ Do you keep your cool during practice?

☐ Do you stay focused when you're in the gym?

☐ Do you practice perfectly?

☐ Do you encourage beginning boxers?

☐ Do you listen respectfully to your coaches?

☐ Do you love hard work?

☐ Do you work on cardiovascular fitness regularly?

☐ Do you eat healthy foods?

☐ Do you approach bouts with confidence and humility?

☐ Do you visualize yourself as a champion?

☐ Do you have respect for all your opponents?

☐ Do you believe you can achieve your goals?

☐ Do you love a challenge?

Chapter One
Fundamentals and Skill Building

Fundamentals and Skill Building

Sound Fundamentals

Don't box if you are lazy, because boxing is a grueling sport. You have to be in top condition to box—you even have to be in pretty good condition just to train as a boxer. When you work on the skills of boxing you must be able to focus on that skill itself. If you do not learn the fundamentals correctly now, you will never learn them. Do not develop bad habits because you don't feel like putting forth the effort or are too tired to do it right (or because you believe everything you see in *Rocky* movies). These excuses for not working correctly inevitably will lead you to failure. Push yourself to always work your movement and throw punches correctly. Your body depends on muscle memory and takes over when your mind falters, so be sure that your body has memorized the correct techniques. You will certainly find times when you are too tired to think in the ring. You won't have to worry about this happening if you practice skills perfectly.

In *The Ultimate Boxer* you will notice that boxing skills are organized a little differently than in most boxing books, or even in the way most coaches teach them. Generally, boxers learn offense first, then later learn defense. However, offense and defense are not independent of each other in competition. It all becomes one fluid motion. As a result, you should learn both skills at the same time, integrating what you know—always practicing both together. Let your offense lead you into defense and let your defense lead you into offense. Your opponent will never see it coming, and it will eventually become second nature to you.

Boxing is not an easy sport. If it were easy, everyone would do it. In

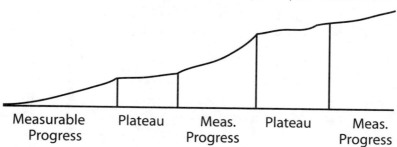

Figure 1.1: The Learning Curve indicates people feel as though they learn rapidly at the beginning of a new technique, followed by a feeling that their ability has leveled off, or even decreased. The cycle of feelings repeats itself throughout the learning process. Knowing this, you should expect some feelings of frustration with your training, but feel confident that they will soon be replaced by feelings of improvement.

reality, only a few make it through the tough workouts. The stance, the punches, even the defense will seem awkward to you at first because it is an unnatural activity. You have to make it become natural, through practice.

Some people progress quickly while others advance more slowly in learning the techniques of boxing. Don't measure your success by others in the gym who may have started training at the same time you did. Remember, in everything there is balance. Some days you will feel strong, coordinated, balanced, quick, alert, and in shape. Other days you will feel like you can't even throw a jab correctly. Learn to take the good with the bad; stay patient and stay focused.

As you critique your own skill, remember to be critical of yourself without defeating yourself. Boxing, like any other sport or activity, has a learning curve (Figure 1.1). At first, you will feel like you learn (and progress) rapidly, then you will plateau until you feel you learn again. Some weeks you will progress rapidly, other weeks you will think you've forgotten everything you thought you had already learned. Stay focused on the process. Take a break, take a breath, and focus again on the fundamentals.

Even though no one "plays boxing" like you play baseball, basketball, soccer, or golf, boxing is fun. If you are not enjoying boxing, then lay off for a while or even try a different sport. If you are not having fun, consider how your attitude might be affecting others in the gym. Stay positive with yourself and with others. Stay balanced in your life and with boxing, and have fun.

> **In everything find balance.**

Make some goals for yourself to keep focused. Why are you boxing? Are you boxing for fitness? Are you boxing for self-defense? Do you want to lose weight? Do you want to box competitively? Do you want to win a state or national title? You must be able to visualize your goals before you can achieve greatness for yourself. You must give yourself something to work toward, and set a plan for action.

When you think of your goals for training and competition, remember to list "S.M.A.R.T." goals. Set goals that are Specific, Measurable, Attainable, Realistic, and Time-bound. Be as specific as possible when you

Fundamentals and Skill Building

write and think about your goals. Keep in mind how you will know when you have reached your goal—what measure will you use to see if you have met a goal. Set goals that are within your reach, and that can be realistically achieved within the set amount of time that you allow. To achieve long-term goals you have to first realize mid-range and short-term goals.

The points of success that get you from your short-term achievements to fulfilling your long-term goals are called mid-range goals. Mid-range goals cover the months ahead, and provide an outline and timeline for reaching your long-term goals. How often will you train? How long can you train? Do you want to spar? How often will you run or do other conditioning programs? Use these goals to chart your progress as you strive to reach your long-term goals.

The short-term goals determine what you will accomplish daily and weekly. What will you work on in your next practice? Which cardiovascular exercise will you complete today? What mental frame of mind will you focus on during practice? Which skills and strategies do you need to learn this week? Short-term goals specify training habits that help you reach your mid-range and long-range goals. They are the steppingstones for building skill and knowledge of boxing.

Long-range, mid-range, and short-term goals work together. If your long-range goal, for example, were to win a regional title, then your mid-range goals might include winning local bouts, working on boxing skills three or four days per week, and completing cardiovascular training six days per week. Your short-term goals might include going to practice three days this week, running in the morning, specifying which skills you still need to learn, and going to practice with a good attitude.

Keep your goals in mind as you learn and practice boxing skills. Write down your goals and post them in your locker, keep them in your

---

What are your goals for boxing?

Long-term goals: _____

Mid-range goals: _____

Short-term goals: _____

gym bag, put them on your bedroom wall, or keep them in your pocket calendar. Use the Goals Worksheet at the back of this book to write more goals for yourself, and set your own action plan. Your goals may change as you progress in your boxing workouts. Revisit your goals often, and rewrite your goals several times each year. Develop a career strategy in much the same way that you develop a ring strategy.

The sport of boxing has been likened to a physical chess match. Boxing is a sport of skill, and each participant attempts to outsmart his/her opponent in a variety of ways. Be sure you learn skills in the gym that will transfer to the competition ring. You should do virtually all of your thinking in the gym so that at the time of competition you can react to openings, counters, defensive moves, and the variety of boxing styles you will meet in your career. Boxing is quick and there are no rests between attacks. Prepare in the gym so you don't have to process during a bout—you can instead focus on responding effectively to all of your opponent's tactics.

You will get out of boxing what you put into it. If you train intensely and correctly, you will increase your skill level. Many talented boxers who don't train regularly are beaten in big matches they thought they would win easily. Boxing never gets boring because you can always improve your skills. Practicing everything the correct way ensures a solid foundation on which you can depend, by building your body's muscle memory.

Boxing has five fundamental punches: #1—jab (lead hand), #2—power punch (strong hand), #3—hook (lead hand), #4—uppercut (strong hand), and #5—uppercut (lead hand). The three fundamental defenses are: hand counters (catching, parrying, blocking), integrative maneuvers (ducking, slipping, sliding, rolling), and directional maneuvers (side stepping, taking angles). All other punches and defensive moves are variations on these fundamentals. For example, the overhand cross is a variation on the #2—power punch. You cannot master the subtleties of variations on punches and defensive moves until you grasp the basics of the fundamentals.

One of the most important exercises to hone your boxing skills and improve your fundamentals is shadowboxing. Shadowboxing is moving—in front of a mirror or in a ring—just like you are boxing an opponent. This means you throw punches like you would in a bout, with full extension and speed. You should move in all directions, all the while imagining your opponent in front of you. Imagine your opponent

Fundamentals and Skill Building

is hitting back, is moving back, to the side, sliding forward. Imagine you have command of the ring, that you are controlling the pace. Imagine yourself comfortable, in control, and strong. Work up a sweat when you shadowbox; get all your muscles warm with this skill-building exercise. Shadowbox with a purpose. What you practice will become habit, so always be sure to practice techniques correctly. Practicing often doesn't make you better, practicing the correct way makes you better. Practice like you want to perform.

Other activites that will improve your overall efficiency as a boxer are hitting bags; using focus mitts (punch pads); practicing one-step, two-step, and directed sparring drills; free-form sparring; and competitive boxing. These exercises will be discussed in greater depth in later chapters.

The exercises outlined in this book are designed to help you become an educated boxer. Practicing and understanding the skills covered in this book will give you an edge over your opponents. Learn all aspects of the sport to be successful. Train so that you are simultaneously ready to attack your opponent and defend against his/her attack. Train with patience, curiosity, and confidence that you are learning skills that will help you become a successful boxer.

You have to practice like a champion to be a champion. If you develop good habits in the gym, you will be able to depend on them in the ring.

Practice does not make perfect.
Perfect practice makes perfect.
Practice your skills perfectly.

Think Feet

Boxer's stance, front view.

Boxers must be able to move with ease in order to elude punches, throw punches correctly, and generate power in their punches. Your feet (and legs) are the first element of your boxing stance. The stance is fundamental to all offensive and defensive movement.

To find your correct stance, stand with your feet shoulder-width apart, then take one step forward with your left leg (if you are right-handed). The lead leg (left leg if you are right-handed) should be in front and to the left of the other leg. Keep your knees slightly bent. This will lower your center of gravity (giving you a more solid base) and make all your movements sharp. If your stance is too wide you will not be able to move quickly. If your stance is too narrow, you will not be balanced when you are hit or when move. Balance your body weight between your legs. Think of your legs as cat-like—always ready to spring in any direction.

Boxer's stance, side view.

Turn your hips slightly to your strong side in order to move your lead shoulder ahead of the other. Bend your legs so that your back foot's heel is off the ground slightly. The front foot should be pointing toward your opponent and your back foot should be pointing at about a thirty-degree angle. Now balance your weight between your legs (as if you're going to sit on a stool placed underneath you) and on the balls of your feet. *Do not* stand on your toes.

Though the weight is focused on the ball of the foot, use the whole front foot for balance. Also make sure your back foot is not directly behind the lead foot (your feet should stay shoulder-width apart). This is the basic stance that most boxers utilize. If you can eventually feel comfortable in this position, you will be able to move in all directions with relative ease. The perfect boxing position is one in which you can move easily, anytime and anywhere, while staying balanced. In this position you can attack, move, defend, or counter without any advance warning to your opponent.

The back heel is off the ground for two reasons: 1) it will keep you in a position so you can move and respond quickly, and 2) you will be able to rotate the back foot when you throw punches with your strong hand. This will allow you to whip the hip in order to generate speed and power.

Fundamentals and Skill Building

The stance will feel awkward for a while. Constantly check your stance in practice to make sure you get it right. Done properly, the stance stresses the calf muscles and gluteus maximus (buttocks), so take care to warm up/stretch all muscles before and after practices.

In a correct stance your arms should be bent at the elbow. Closed fists should rest at cheek level, with the lead hand (the left for right-handers) slightly ahead of the other. The thumb of your strong-side glove may touch your face, and your palms should be facing each other. Close your hands, but don't hold them tightly. Wrists stay straight, and chin stays tucked into your chest. Imagine you are looking at your opponent through your eyebrows.

Turn the waist so the lead shoulder (left, if you are right-handed) is ahead. Leading with the shoulder has several advantages. First, your reach is longer since your shoulder is extended toward the opponent. Second, the time to your target is reduced dramatically since you are beginning with a head start. Third, you can generate tort with your waist when you choose to throw your cross. Fourth, the jab is more difficult to read, since the shoulder is already prepped. Fifth, the lead arm can quickly defend the head or body against attack. This positioning with the legs and hands is known as "on-guard" position, and it is your basic stance.

Footwork

Footwork is the basis for boxing. Practicing good footwork is crucial. You will need to perfect four basic movements: advancing (moving forward), retreating (moving backward), moving laterally (right and left), and pivoting (a circular movement). The foot closest to the

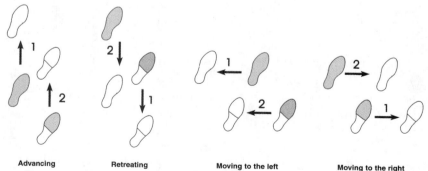

Figure 1.2: The foot closest to the direction in which you are moving should always move first. Never cross your feet when moving.

direction you are going moves first (Figure 1.2).

If you are going to the right, move your right leg first. If you are moving backward, move your back leg first. Never cross your feet in front of each other. Doing so will make you lose your balance or tangle up your feet. Stay in your stance while you move in order to maintain balance while you are in motion. Don't think of moving as taking steps. Push off the back (trail) foot in order to get to your destination quickly. The trail foot will move as much as the lead foot, so if you move forward six inches with the lead foot, then your trail leg will move forward six inches, finishing in the correct boxing stance (and on balance). Small movements are sufficient. Don't try to cover ground quickly by taking huge steps; doing so may throw off your balance.

Why push off instead of step? If you get in the habit of stepping, eventually you will start walking around the ring, and thus allow the heel to strike first (like it would if you were walking down the street). If the heel strikes first, you are not in a balanced stance. You cannot move well with your heel, you cannot change directions with the heel, you are off balance if you get hit while you are striking with your heel, and you bring your center of gravity higher if you strike the canvas with the heel. It is an entirely inefficient boxing movement. The push-off, on the other hand, will give you power because it will help keep you in a good stance as you move quickly and powerfully.

The push-off should feel as though you are gliding across the canvas. By keeping your feet on the canvas at all times, you will be ready to react to your opponent. Keep movement efficient so that your reaction time is quick.

Pivoting is simply leaving your lead foot in place as you spin your trail foot (and body) around to the right or left. To pivot, imagine you have a sandbag on the toes of your lead foot, but you want to move your body away from your opponent. Spin away while still maintaining the same amount of distance to your opponent (Figure 1.3). Your lead foot will move a little (it has to in order to accommodate your opponent). The pivot is easiest to practice on the maze ball, double-end bag, or heavy bag. The pivot is most effective when used in conjunction with a duck, or while you are throwing a combination in order to change the angle of attack.

Good boxing position (also known as the "on-guard" position) aligns the feet, legs, hips, shoulders, arms, hands, head, and chin. Use the exercises below to improve your footwork. Practice these drills

Fundamentals and Skill Building

slowly, gradually speeding up movements, until you develop sound technique. Reguarly check your form in a mirror.

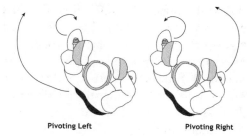

Pivoting Left   Pivoting Right

Figure 1.3: Pivoting to the left and right requires turning the lead foot as the body spins.

EXERCISES TO INCREASE MOBILITY:
1. Stretch and move around to increase your heart rate
2. Mirror work: four rounds of three minutes = advance, retreat, move to the right, to the left, and pivot
3. Ring work: four rounds of three minutes = advance, retreat, move to the right, to the left, and pivot

If you are a beginner, always focus a few rounds on footwork before you start to incorporate punches into your footwork drills. Stay balanced and do not overextend on any of your punches. If you miss your target you should still be in a good boxing stance, ready to move or to throw another punch.

FOOTWORK WITH PUNCHING EXERCISES:
1. Advance and retreat throwing the...
   - jab
   - cross
   - jab and cross in a combination
2. Lateral moves (to the right or left) throwing the...
   - jab
   - cross
   - jab and cross in a combination
3. Pivoting (right and left) throwing the...
   - jab
   - cross
   - jab and cross in a combination

REMINDERS FOR GOOD FOOTWORK:
- Keep your legs bent.
- Keep your back heel off the ground.
- Balance your weight between your legs — concentrated on the balls of your feet; be ready to attack or protect yourself on defense.
- Push off your back foot to move forward. Don't let the front heel strike first (the ball of the front foot should catch your momentum).
- Keep your chin tucked.
- Stay balanced.

> **Footwork makes the punch.**

The Hands and Punching Reminders

The arms and hands deliver punches to the target and provide the last line of defense against an opponent's blows. Though a boxer's arsenal includes many different punches, offensive tactics have ten important elements in common:

1) The hands should always stay in the on-guard position, unless you are throwing a punch or moving the hands for defensive maneuvers. When the hands are up, they can be turned easily to parry punches or be deployed quickly to deliver a scoring blow. Additionally, when the hands are always up, it is difficult for your opponent to anticipate when you might be throwing a punch. Boxers that move their hands up or down to throw punches are easy to read, and thus easy to defend. Also, when the hands are in the on-guard position, the elbows are close to the body, in "pockets" near the ribs. In this way, the elbows can protect the stomach and allow the fists to rest comfortably in front of the face.

2) When throwing a straight punch, such as the jab and power punch, the fist remains upright until the end of the punch. All straight punches should "snap." The snap occurs when the fist is turned over so that the first two knuckles of the hand dig into the target. To accomplish this snapping action, keep the fist positioned so that the

Figure 1.4: The fist turns over before impact, and the thumb is closed to the fist.

Fundamentals and Skill Building

thumb is pointed toward the ceiling while you extend the arm. When your arm is 95 percent extended, turn the fist over so the thumb is to the side. Finally, at the end of the extension, the knuckles can be rotated so the knuckles of the pointer and middle fingers dig into the target (Figure 1.4).

Once thrown, a punch must return straight back to the on-guard position. A fast return helps protect the head and prepares the hand to be thrown again. The arm should not be fully extended on any punch, especially straight punches, since it can easily hyperextend if you miss the target. A punch "ends" when it is back in its starting position (with the fist at the cheek). Stay relaxed and snap the hand back to the cheek rapidly.

Figure 1.5: Straight punches are thrown so that the first two knuckles create a direct line of sight.

3) Throwing effective punches involves the use of basic geometry: the shortest distance between two points is a straight line. The fastest and hardest punch travels in a straight line. Imagine your fist travels this straight line and then returns on the same plane (Figure 1.5). To prove the point to yourself, find someone who loops their punches and practice throwing straight jabs and power punches when you see their shoulder move in preparation to throw a punch. A straight punch will always beat a looped punch.

4) Punch with a specific target in sight. Aim for the target, and try to punch one or two inches beyond it. When connecting with the target—whether its a heavy bag, focus mitt, or opponent—be sure to punch through the target, not at it.

5) Throw all punches with authority, with the purpose of contacting your intended target. Don't get caught throwing lazy punches. Lazy punches are slow, they are usually dropped as they are thrown, they stay on the target too long, and they return to the on-guard position slowly and/or low. Lazy punches, especially lazy jabs, are easy for opponents to parry and counter. Conversely, don't try to muscle punches to the target; stay relaxed and focused. Muscling punches requires tension in the muscles, slowing the action of the arm. Throw punches with authority, not muscle. A stealth punch

Figure 1.6: The chin is always tucked when throwing punches.

(easily thrown, not turning over until the extension) is also difficult to detect, thus making it harder to defend.

6) Keep the chin tucked close to the chest with every punch. The shoulder may actually contact the cheek when the fist is turned over at the extension of jabs and straight crosses. Tucking the chin and rotating the fist will serve to protect the chin and jaw. (Figure 1.6)

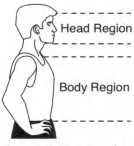

Figure 1.7: Upstairs and downstairs target zones.

7) The boxer targets two zones: the head and the body (Figure 1.7). The head, also referred to as "upstairs," includes the sides or front of the head. The body, also known as "downstairs," is comprised of the chest, stomach, and ribs. You may not contact an opponent on top or back of the head or neck, on the back, or below the belt line. When punching, remember to punch through a variety of targets in the upstairs and downstairs zones. Mixing up the zones keeps the opponent off guard and makes your punches more difficult to defend.

8) Another important element in an effective punch is the positioning of the legs and body. Always keep the body behind the knee when throwing punches. Centering and balancing the body supports punches and defensive maneuvers. A lower center of gravity generates more force for punches and steadies the body to better withstand blows.

9) Breathing should remain constant when boxing. Extending the arm out to throw the punch is considered the exertion part of the movement. Exhaling as you throw punches will help work through the exertion point. You are also more vulnerable while punching. Exhaling through the punch will contract the stomach muscles, which may aid your ability to withstand an opponent's punch.

10) Finally, punch when your opponent is within range. Don't waste energy throwing punches that you know will not connect. Save your punches for testing distance or scoring blows. Stay ready to throw punches when your opponent is within range. If you don't punch, your opponent will.

Boxer readiness is the mental and physical position in which you can attack and defend against attack.

The Jab and Duck

The jab is the most important punch. The jab measures the distance between you and your opponent; it sets up other punches; and it improves the efficiency of your defense. The majority of punches thrown are jabs; in fact, more than 80 percent of your punches (and your opponent's punches) will be jabs. So be ready (be physically conditioned) to throw them, and be ready to guard against them, because your opponent will be throwing jabs, too. In the proper boxer's stance, the jab is quick and smooth. You should be prepared to throw 200 jabs in a three-minute round of shadow boxing. We will call the jab the "number one" punch, noted as #1.

From your boxer's stance, begin the jab by shooting your fist toward the target. Keep your elbow in the pocket as the fist moves forward. When your arm is 95 percent extended, turn the fist over so that the thumb is to the side and the first two knuckles dig into the target.

Stay relaxed with the punch (don't muscle it to the target), and throw the jab with authority. Bring the jab back in the same straight line in which you threw it. If you lower it on its way back to the starting position your opponent will recognize this as a pattern and will take advantage of your careless habit. The jab is a critical punch. Take great care to learn to throw it correctly.

The jab's power is achieved with the body. Push off the back leg (without moving the foot) to provide momentum in order to snap the lead shoulder slightly forward as your arm extends.

Jabbing to the body (stomach region) requires bending your legs to deliver the blow. From this position you can maintain correct technique. Many boxers jab to the body by simply aiming lower, but this lazy jab will leave your head exposed and will travel slowly.

Whether jabbing to the head or body, remember to punch in a straight line so your rotated shoulder protects your jaw and so you don't leave openings around your head. Make your target (on bags or in the mirror) always a little higher than your shoulder so you become accustomed to throwing high, and you properly rotate the fist and shoulder.

Throwing a jab on the heavy bag.

The jab is the one punch that can be thrown effectively from any position and while you are moving. The jab doesn't require the same leverage that the other punches require. Use the jab as you move back, forward, while pivoting, ducking, side stepping, and even while walking away. "Sticking" a jab is the act of forcing an opponent to retreat due to a stiff jab. Connecting with a jab and then moving out of range of the opponent's punches is known as the "stick and move," and is a very popular technique. When the jab is the last punch thrown in a combination it helps reinstate a balanced position, and also keeps your opponent at bay since you have more extension with the jab than with any other punch.

Throwing a jab to the body requires bending the legs.

If you ever doubt which punch to throw in a bout, throw the jab. Typically you should try to throw more than one jab at a time. Defending against single jabs is easy; defending against a series of jabs is difficult. Try throwing two or three jabs at your opponent while moving and setting up combinations.

While the jab is an effective punch for scoring points and for probing the opponent to check proper distance, it is also effective in disrupting your opponent's attack, or in keeping the opponent on defense so that he/she does not attempt to throw punches. With a strong jab you can control the bout and keep your opponent frustrated.

Defending against the jab

The defense against a jab to the head is the catch/parry, duck, slip, half-step back and side step. The defense against a jab to the body is a block with the elbow or half-step back.

The boxer with the best jab usually wins the bout.

The Duck

The duck is an easy defense: simply bend your legs to allow punches to go over your head. Allow very little clearance so you can quickly pop back into your boxing stance. As in Figure 1.8, imagine a line running down the center of your body, and duck so that your weight stays balanced on either side of the line.

Figure 1.8: The legs are bent quickly, and the body drops straight down when ducking.

In your boxer's stance, practice dropping your weight (by bending your legs and slightly bending forward at the waist). This should be an explosive movement as you pop back up into your stance. If you stay down too long you will become a target. Keep your eyes on your opponent as you duck—you should always be able to see the hands of your opponent. If you cannot see your opponent's hands and chest, then you may be bending too low. Also, remember to keep your hands up in your guard position as you duck. The duck can be used effectively against jabs, crosses, and hooks thrown to the head.

Do not bend your waist too much when ducking. Many boxers, because they are out of shape, bend at the waist instead of the knees. You can check for this by looking in the mirror at your lowest point. Can you see yourself? Can you see your opponent's punches? If you can't see your opponent's punches, then you may be bending your waist too much. If you can't see what's coming, you will not be able to defend yourself or score blows. Bending too much at the waist, often called "tipping your hat," is also a foul in amateur boxing. Referees will warn against this infraction and may even stop the bout if they think you are fouling because you are exhausted or overwhelmed.

Tipping your hat, ducking too low, and staying down too long are movements that waste time and energy and are dangerous. It is also difficult to throw punches from these positions. A well executed duck should move you out of harm's way and propel you into an offensive attack.

The duck can easily incorporate a jab to the body.

EXERCISES FOR THE JAB AND DUCK:
1. Warm up and practice footwork first.
2. Add the jab to your footwork—move with one jab at a time.
3. Move and then throw two jabs.
4. Move and jab at the same time.
5. Duck and jab to the body simultaneously
6. Jab to the body, and then jab to the head.

REMINDERS FOR THE JAB AND DUCK:
- Keep your legs bent.
- Keep your chin down.
- Keep your wrist straight.
- Extend your arm only 98 percent.
- Turn the punch over at the "snap."
- Exhale as you extend your punches.
- Stay balanced.

When in doubt, throw a jab.

Fundamentals and Skill Building

The Cross and Slip/Slide

The right cross (or the left cross for a left-hander) is considered the power punch. It is also known the #2 punch, the power punch, or the strong-side punch. This punch moves down the line of your shoulder, and uses the tort of your body's hip and shoulder thrust to propel it outward. The cross usually follows a jab, because the jab is used to measure the distance to the opponent, or even to make an opening for the power hand. Two basic types of cross are the short cross and the power punch.

Throw the cross straight from the cheek to the target, and then straight back to the cheek. From your boxer's stance, begin the cross by rotating your back foot (on the ball of the foot)—which will turn the knee, which will turn the hip, which will turn the shoulder—and then shoot your fist toward the target. Driving the rear leg is the most important step in throwing the cross, because it is this foot that begins the whole process. Rotation on the back leg provides "pop" to the punch.

Your body's weight will shift onto the lead leg as you throw your power hand. Just as you did with the jab, keep your elbow in when throwing the cross by keeping the fist up (thumb toward the ceiling). As your arm approaches full extension, turn the fist over, and then snap the punch back to its starting position. Stay relaxed with the punch (don't muscle it to the target), but throw it quick and straight.

For the cross to be thrown quickly, it must travel in a straight line. Imagine that this line extends from your cheek (where the fist rests) to the target. Force your glove to travel that imaginary line. Return on that imaginary line to get the punch back in defense quickly as well.

Rotating the hips helps rotate the shoulder when throwing the cross—providing reach and power.

Whether throwing to the head or body, remember to throw and retract the punch in a straight line. Make your target (on bags or in the mirror) always a little higher than your nose so that you get in the habit of rotating your fist and shoulder over to protect your chin. Also, keep your lead hand in position when you throw the cross, so that you are prepared to defend yourself if your opponent throws at the same time. Throwing the power punch can leave you vulnerable, since it has farther to travel than a punch thrown with the lead shoulder. Make all punches crisp and straight.

The Short Cross

The fastest, and perhaps most devastating, cross is the short cross (also known as the "quick cross"). This cross

Figure 1.9: Throwing a straight right cross to the body on the heavy bag.

is thrown quickly and without much power. The idea is to score and tag your opponent, not to knock him/her out. However, a quick cross is often a knockout punch precisely because it is thrown quickly (so it's not seen), and because it is thrown straight it generates more power than other punches, such as the hook.

The short cross is most useful when you are too close to an opponent to generate full range of the power hand, and when you need to punch or score quickly. The quick cross is able to deliver speed without telegraphing the punch to your opponent. The short cross shoots out without warning, similar to the jab, then sneaks past defense and connects to the chin. It is usually followed by another punch, such as the jab. For right-handers, the short right can be an effective lead against left-handers.

The Power Cross

The power cross is the punch with which most people are familiar. This is the punch that has the most power behind it, though ironically it is thrown the same way as the quick cross. The only difference is that the power cross draws more support and power from the feet. The push and rotation of the back (right) foot, knee, hip, and shoulder is imperative. Arm punches cannot be thrown as powerfully as a punch that is thrown with the body behind it.

The cross is often the most readable of all punches because the thrower telegraphs the punch by cocking the shoulder, planting both feet, or even grimacing. Don't give away such a valuable weapon: practice throwing the cross in the mirror so you eventually throw it with ease and without a hint of what is to come. Throw the power cross under control, in case you miss. Finally, finish the punch by drawing it back to its original position, so you are ready to defend or throw again.

Punching to the stomach area requires that you bend your knees to

Fundamentals and Skill Building

bring your shoulder down to the same plane as your target. When extended properly, this movement protects the chin and allows you to rotate the hips. Make sure you also keep the lead hand in defensive position (Figure 1.9).

Defending against the cross

The defense against a right cross is to parry with the left hand, smother the punch with a block, block with the shoulder, roll away from the punch, duck, slide to the outside, or sidestep the punch. The most common defense for the right hand to the head (by another right-hander) is the block, where the back of the left glove is placed against the forehead to absorb the blow. When the punch connects, the receiver "gives" with the punch (letting the bent legs move the body slightly backward), displacing the force of the blow and allowing it to hit the back of the left glove. The most common defense of the cross to the body is to block with the elbow or take a half-step back.

The Slip and Slide

The slip and slide are used when you desire to avoid your opponent's punches without moving completely out of range. The slip involves simply twisting the body and leaning over your strong-side leg by slightly bending your legs. The slide is the slipping action toward the other side. Like the duck, you want very little clearance as the punches move past your ears. The slip is used against your opponent's jab. In a right-handed stance, if your opponent throws a right-hand, then you should slide to your left. Slip (or slide) by moving to the outside of your opponent's attack, not to the inside where he or she can hit you easily with their other hand.

You can slip/slide straight punches such as the #1 or #2 punches. The slip/slide also can be combined with other defensive moves, such as the duck. For example, you can slip a jab, then duck under a hook.

In your boxer's stance, practice twisting your waist and dropping your weight (turn the shoulders and bend your legs while moving your weight slightly over the thigh of either leg). This should be a very quick movement. Do not stay over too long, and do not go from one side to the other while down low. Staying

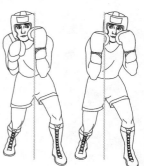

The slip and slide twist and bend the body outside of the center line.

down in front of your opponent will make the top of your head a target.

Do not slip simply by bending your waist. Doing so will "tip your hat," and you will be hit because this is a slow action. Watching in the mirror, check your position in the middle of the slip. Your body should be directly over the leg and slightly forward—not to the side, and not leaning back. A good position on the slip/slide will keep you in the zone for offensive strikes. In the middle of your slip, you should be able to throw a jab while staying on balance.

Do not stay over to the side for long when you slip—make it quick. Either pop back into your original stance, or move. Staying over to the side too long gives your opponent time to hit you. Moving over too much is wasted motion, and if you are hit in this position you will likely go down for lack of balance. A good slip will propel you straight into an offensive strike. Moving off of the slip can be accomplished with either a pivot or a side step. Some slips also can turn into ducks if done quickly. Most importantly, keep your hands in on-guard position when slipping. Though the body moves faster if one hand is down, you leave yourself exposed if you do. Practice correctly all the time and the slip/slide will become one of your most valuable defenses.

EXERCISES FOR THE CROSS AND SLIP/SLIDE:
1. Warm up and practice footwork first.
2. Add the jab to your mirror footwork or in the ring—move while throwing one jab at a time.
3. Move around the ring throwing just the left and right shoulders.
4. Move around the ring only throwing quick crosses.
5. Throw #1 and #2 punches after moving.
6. Throw a double #1, and then a #2.
7. Slip then jab and throw a #2.
8. Slip and slide, throwing the #2 simultaneously with the slide.
9. Move, double #1 and slip, then #2, then move.
10. Move with a slip, then #1 downstairs and throw a #2 upstairs.

REMINDERS FOR THE CROSS AND SLIP/SLIDE:
- Keep your legs bent.
- Keep your chin down.
- Turn over the punch at the "snap."
- Let the back foot turn sharply on the ball of the foot, digging it into the floor for leverage.

Fundamentals and Skill Building

- Drive your hips around quickly.
- Let your shoulder rotate as you extend your arm.
- Extend and return the punch on the same plane.
- Let your shoulder knuckle rotate up to protect the chin.
- Exhale on the punch.
- Stay balanced.

Straight punches travel faster than looped ones.

The Hook, Parry/Catch, and Block

The hook, also known as the #3 punch, is a sneaky weapon. Unlike all other punches, the hook travels a curve, so it is able to move around a defensive guard. The curve also means that the punch sometimes goes undetected, since it moves quickly outside your opponent's peripheral vision. This is the reason boxers get hurt by the hook—they don't see it coming.

The three basic types of hooks are: the lead or long-range hook, the mid-range hook, and the short-range or inside hook. Each type has its own merits.

The lead (or long-range) hook can be particularly deceptive. Most opponents will only expect jabs to be thrown at long range. When they commit to the defense of a jab (such as catching it), they leave themselves open to be struck by a long-range hook.

Mid-range hooks are meant to strike when you are in the boxing zone. This hook has the most power since you are in good range and are far enough away to get a good turn on your body (to increase the momentum of the strike). The mid-range hook will serve you well when you have your opponent on the ropes or in the corner. Don't smother your opponent; keep proper distance so you can snap your punches.

Short hooks are for infighting, when you are crouched close to your opponent. These hooks are tight and snap at the follow-through, rather than move through the target. They are designed to catch your opponent off guard by sneaking past gloves and finding openings. You also can throw a hard hook inside by whipping the left hip to turn the arm quickly. If you do this, be sure to keep the strong side defended, since you will be particularly vulnerable to attack.

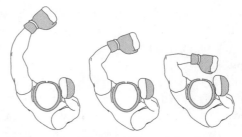

Bird's-eye view of lead, middle, and short hooks.

To throw a left hook (if you are right-handed), start with your weight slightly on your lead leg (left leg). Rotate your body on the lead foot so that your weight is on the ball of the lead foot. As you pivot your foot, knee, hip, and shoulder, and move the weight to the back leg, turn the hand over so that the palm is facing the floor. Bring the elbow behind the punch to maximize its force. Throw through the target, and end the punch back in good boxing position.

Drive through your target about two inches, and stay under control, so that you minimize your vulnerabilities if you miss. Keep your balance.

When throwing a body hook, be certain to lower your own body so that the punch is delivered at about shoulder level. Maintain the strong-side arm's defensive position when you throw a hook to the head or the body.

Defending against the hook

Defensive strategies for the hook include blocking it, ducking, taking a half-step back, and smothering it. Blocking a left hook is accomplished by raising the hand to the ear so it completely covers the

Throwing a hook to the head on the heavybag. The lead foot pivots in order to turn the hip.

Fundamentals and Skill Building

side of the head. However, a more effective defense is to evade the hook by ducking it, and then quickly moving into your own offensive attack. The half-step back is also effective, but should be used with caution. Smothering the hook involves bringing your body closer to your opponent's in order to stay inside of where the hook would otherwise land. Defending the body hook is easily accomplished with an elbow block. The single best defense for a hook is to circle away from it (for example, avoid a right-hander's left hook by circling to your left).

A hook can also be thrown as you take an angle against your opponent.

The Parry/Catch

The parry (or catch) is probably the easiest defense because it does not require that you move your body—you only move the hand that is catching the punch. However, if you do not catch correctly, it can be the most dangerous of all defenses.

First, imagine that your elbows sit in pockets when you are in your boxing stance. When you catch a punch to your head, do not let your elbows come out of their pockets. Second, catching only involves rotating the wrist 45 degrees so that you catch the knuckles of the opposition's glove into the palm of your receiving hand. Third, leave the glove at your chin where you wait for the punch to meet you.

Do not reach for your opponent's glove! If you reach, and miss, you leave yourself wide open to be hit. A good boxer will utilize the feint in hopes of getting you to reach (or "paw" at the punch), and then strike you with either hand. Pawing at punches is a common mistake, so practice making yourself wait on the punch before you catch it. Don't fall victim to feints.

The parry requires turning the palm to catch the knuckles of the opponent's glove.

Once you master the catch, you can start to manipulate it. Parrying a punch means that you move it away (by deflecting and/or catching and redirecting it). You move the opponent's fist down, to the inside, or to the outside. If you can control where your opponent's hand is, then you can easily capitalize on the openings that you have created. Does your opponent throw a lazy jab? Does your opponent lower the right hand to throw the left? Remember that catching and parrying happens fast. Be purposeful in your parrying without being slow.

Right-handers catch the jab of another right-hander in their right palm. Doing this keeps the left hand available to jab back at the opponent, either during the catch or immediately after it. Your left will have a longer reach and you can counter attack with either a jab or a long-range hook to your opponent's head.

Parry of opponent's jab.

The Block

Blocking is a defensive move in which you attempt to 1) prevent the opponent's glove from cleanly contacting a scoring portion of your head or body, or 2) displace the force of the blow. The block is accomplished by placing the back of the glove, the shoulder, or the elbow/forearm in the path of the punch. Blocking, also called absorbing and guarding, a blow is most effective if the torso is moved or twisted in the direction that the punch is traveling, at the same time the punch lands, thus reducing the impact.

Straight punches to the head, such as the straight right, are blocked with the back of the glove. Hooks to the head may be blocked with the back of the glove or the shoulder (by rotating it up to guard the chin).

Right-handers catch a right cross with the back of their left glove and give with the legs to take the power off of the punch. To block the cross, touch the knuckles of your lead hand to your forehead. Keep your chin tucked and elbow in. When the punch meets your glove, bend slightly at the waist and knees to deflect the force of the punch. After your opponent's cross makes contact, immediately throw a short cross in

Blocking the right cross with the back of the left glove.

Blocking with the shoulder.

Fundamentals and Skill Building

return, beating his/her punch to its defensive position.

Body shots are blocked with the elbow, since lowering your glove would leave one side of your head vulnerable to attack. When blocking a body blow, be sure to slightly tighten the abdominal muscles as you absorb the punch with your elbow. Tightening the muscles will help protect your torso in case the punch actually connects.

Blocking with the elbow.

EXERCISES FOR THE HOOK AND PARRY/CATCH:
1. Warm up and practice footwork first.
2. Move around the ring throwing just the left and right shoulders.
3. Work on just the hook: lead hook, middle range hook, close hook.
4. Throw #2 and #3 punches after moving.
5. Catch and #3 (simultaneously)
6. Catch and #1 (simultaneously), then long #3.
7. Throw a #1, #2, #3 to body, #3 to head, pivot out.
8. Duck and #3 to body, then #2 and #1 on the move.

REMINDERS FOR THE HOOK AND THE PARRY/CATCH:
- Keep your knees bent.
- Pivot your front foot on the ball.
- Drive your hips around quickly.
- Shift your weight from the front leg to the back leg during the punch.
- Make your arm and shoulder move together.
- Keep your elbow behind the punch.
- Keep your opposite hand pinned to your head.
- Keep your chin tucked.
- Stay balanced.

Efficient punching depends on total alignment of the body.

The Uppercuts and Half-Step Back

Uppercuts, also known as the #4 (strong hand) and #5 (lead hand) punches, can be devastating punches. Uppercuts travel in straight lines, but come from below the defense, rather than right at it. Uppercuts are best used against boxers who lead with their head, or while boxing within very close range of your opponent.

To throw a proper uppercut, use your body to throw the punch. Bend the knees (and waist slightly) to position your gloves lower than the target. Keep your gloves in defensive position while you lower your body and shift your body weight slightly to the side of the body that will deliver the blow. The arms should remain in half-bent positions, and palms should face each other. Then quickly explode up with your legs, turn the palm so it is facing you, and whip the fist to the target (either the chin or solar plexus). Don't drop the hand to throw the uppercut, use your body to get good position and add power to the punch. To follow with another uppercut, simply lower the legs again and explode up with the opposite hand. Be sure to keep the non-throwing hand in good position for defensive purposes. Punch through your target and return your hand immediately to its starting position.

An uppercut uses the power of the legs, and can surprise an opponent.

The uppercut is most useful when it stops a fast-approaching jab, or when it threads the needle on the inside of a good defense. Most good boxers are prepared to stop jabs, crosses, and hooks, but few know how to stop a good uppercut to the body or the head.

Uppercuts can be thrown both long-range and inside. Long-range uppercuts almost look like jabs, but turn under rather than over at the last moment. The long-range uppercut can be effective against opponents who only expect to defend against jabs. The inside uppercuts are used when you are in middle range or infighting with your opponent, especially against someone who bends at the waist too much. The uppercut can follow any punch

Throwing a right uppercut on the heavy bag.

and can transition into any punch.

If you have your opponent on the ropes, be sure to mix your uppercuts with other punches, such as hooks, to keep your opponent guessing. Don't smother your uppercuts.

Throwing a right uppercut to the body on the heavy bag.

Keep proper distance to maximize your punching power.

Defending against uppercuts

Defense for the uppercuts include: catch (dropping your glove inward and downward), the half-step back, and the side step. Uppercuts to the body can be blocked with either forearm.

Half-Step Back

The half-step back.

The half-step back defense is sneaky and effective, but should be practiced repeatedly before attempting to use it in sparring or in competition. The half-step back involves literally moving only the back foot away from the opponent in an effort to move out of range of the opponent's punch, and then pushing forward to get in boxing position or to explode into your own attack. This defense may be dangerous if you misread your opponent, and fail to elude his/her attack. Also, if you explode forward incorrectly, you can move into an oncoming punch. When done correctly, however, the half-step back is quick, efficient, and difficult to read. The half-step back is most useful against a boxer who has a short reach or who does not advance when throwing punches.

Keep your hands up when you use the half-step back in case your opponent is within range to make contact. Throw your follow-up punch with authority, but stay in good position when you do. A good follow-up punch is the short power punch or the uppercut. The jab and hook also can be thrown with ease after a half-step back.

EXERCISES FOR THE UPPERCUTS:
1. Warm up and practice footwork first.
2. Move around the ring throwing only the left and right shoulders.
3. Work on just the uppercuts: both hands, head and body shots inside and long-range.
4. Throw a #1 and then #4 to the head or the body.
5. Throw a #1, #4, #5.
6. Throw a #1, #4, #3.
7. Throw a #1, #4, #5, #3.
8. Time a #4 against a straight jab.

EXERCISES FOR HALF-STEP BACK:
1. Practice quick half-step backs, pushing off the back leg to explode into position to throw a #1 or a #2.
2. Half-step back, follow with a #2.
3. Catch an imaginary opponent's jab, half-step back as opponent throws a #2, and throw a short #2 when back into position.
4. Throw a #1, parry imaginary opponent's jab, half-step back (imagine opponent throwing a cross), #2.
5. Shoot a #1 and a long-range #3, half-step back, then a #2 and a jab.

REMINDERS FOR UPPERCUTS AND HALF-STEP BACK:
- "Sit down" for power, explosiveness, and balance on uppercuts.
- Turn palm toward your face when throwing.
- Always keep hands in front of your body.
- Keep your gloves on your cheek or chin—don't dip the gloves for leverage.
- Explode with the legs to get power on the punches.
- Make your legs, arms, and shoulders move together.
- Keep the opposite hand pinned to your head.
- Keep your chin down.
- Stay balanced.

Punch placement is the key to scoring.

The Feint, Draw, and Side Step

The feint is the most effective way to deceive your opponent. Feint with the eyes, shoulders, hands, legs, knees, feet, even by making a noise (like exhaling or grunting). Do not always use the same feint, or for the same purpose. Throwing feints can be predictable if done too often, or if done the same way repeatedly. Feint for three basic reasons:

1) To assess how your opponent will react to a punch
2) To make your opponent think, hesitate, or stop his/her attack
3) To make your opponent do something that you want him/her to do (called *drawing*).

Feinting Offense and Movement

Think of the offensive feint as throwing a quarter of a punch that you want to telegraph. With the feint, you are trying to get a reaction from your opponent, such as a cover-up, a retreat, or a counter punch. Feint a punch (like the jab, power punch, or hook) with your arm, and instead throw a different punch, or move to get a better angle for your attack. You can also feint with the lower body by bending the knee quickly as if you are coming forward to attack; or feint a side step, and then punch or use another defensive move to gain an advantage. Your opponent may focus on your movement, and thus leave an opening.

Drawing

Another kind of feint involves intentionally leaving an opening. Drawing is the attempt to trick your opponent into throwing the lead punch that you want him/her to throw. For example, if you carry your hands low, your opponent will probably lead with a jab to the chin. To draw the left lead specifically, carry your right hand lower than usual. A low left hand may successfully draw a right to the head. If you want your opponent to punch you to the body, raise your elbows, the right elbow to draw a left to the body, and raise your left elbow to draw your opponent's right hand to the body. Prepare to counter before you leave the opening. Counter as soon as your opponent is drawn in. But beware, your opponent may realize your intention and may feint at your draw!

Use mirror work to sharpen your feints. In order to test whether your feint is convincing, practice all feints with someone of equal or better skill. Although the feint is useful against anyone, it is especially effective against counterpunchers (opponents who rarely lead). Though good boxers will not fall for feints as often as novice boxers, feints keep your opponent thinking. A distracted opponent is less likely to strike.

Defending against the feint

The most effective defense against the feint is, of course, not to fall for it. You do this by always staying in good boxing position and always being on guard. Don't automatically attack when you think you see a good opening—always remain under control when you want to capitalize on openings you see (or think you see). When you box someone who feints often, respond by stopping the action, and throw an offensive feint back at him/her occasionally.

The Side Step (or Taking an Angle)

The side step is an underrated, under-used defensive tactic that gives you a significant advantage. The side step creates an angle. Though this is an evasive move that keeps you from being hit, it also sets up an attack because you have a better position from which to make contact.

Step to your right most of the time against a right-hander, or left against a left-hander. Doing so will keep you away from your opponent's power punch. Never cross your feet when you are stepping to either side.

A side step for defense can quickly turn into an offensive attack.

EXERCISES TO PRACTICE THE FEINT AND SIDE STEP:

1. Warm up and practice footwork first.
2. Move around the ring throwing only the left and right shoulders.
3. Practice feinting in the mirror—is it believable?
4. Feint a #1 to the head, and throw a #1 to the head or body.
5. Feint a #1, and throw a #2.
6. Feint a #1, and throw a #3 (long-range).
7. Feint a #1, side step and throw a #1 simultaneously.
8. Throw a #1, feint a #2 to the body, and throw #3 to body and head.
9. Jab, sidestep to the left, and throw #2.
10. Feint a long #3, take a half-step back, and counter with a #2 or #1.

REMINDERS FOR THE FEINT AND THE SIDE STEP:
- Keep your knees bent in good boxing position.
- Keep your chin down.
- Use your whole body to feint, not just the arms.
- Follow a feint quickly with offense or defense.
- Keep your gloves in good defensive position when feinting.
- Read your opponent to figure out which feint would work best.
- Make the side step explosive, don't walk.
- Stay balanced.

Infighting, Covering, and Offensive Reminders

Infighting is the practice of staying close to your opponent while still working various punches and defensive maneuvers. Infighting can sometimes appear to be holding because the boxers are close to each other and may even lean on each other. With infighting, boxers actively vye for position, move defensively, and punch.

The main point to remember when infighting is to relax. Infighting takes time and patience. You must shorten your punches to score inside, since there isn't room to fully extend punches. Make punches short and tight so they strike quickly and cleanly. If you want power, take a half-step or full-step back to get good range and extension on your punches.

Keep yourself well covered up while infighting. Your opponent needs only to touch you cleanly to score a blow, so remember to stay in good defensive position while you throw combinations.

Don't use infighting to rest. Use infighting as an opportunity to gain momentum for an offensive attack, or to change the tempo of a bout. Finesse will win bouts, but it takes practice.

Defending against infighting

The best defense for infighting is to keep your hands up and slip, slide, duck, bob, and weave as you work inside with your opponent, so that you are defending yourself while attacking. You can also defend against individual punches that you encounter; this skill will take time to perfect. If your opponent overwhelms you with an inside attack, you can retreat backward or sidestep to get away, or you may also use the cover-up defense, discussed below.

Covering

Covering up is used when all else fails: for example, when you are pinned in the corner or on the ropes. The cover literally means that you cover your face and partially the side of your head with your gloves as you bend your knees and waist slightly in order to also protect your body. Your opponent will still strike you, but his/her punches should land on your gloves or arms. The cover takes some skill because you must be careful to protect yourself without exposing your head or body to attack. Additionally, the cover is often a signal to your opponent that you are hurt, and a skilled opponent will use a covered boxer to his or her advantage. Finally, the cover can be considered passive by a referee who may issue a foul to you and/or stop the bout believing you are hurt. The best aspect of the cover, is the ability to protect yourself and then immediately counterpunch when the opponent leaves an opening.

Covering

REMINDERS WHEN THROWING ALL PUNCHES:
- Finish punches back in their starting position—don't stay extended.
- Relax the arm on the way back to starting position. This will get it back quicker and help conserve energy.
- Punch through the target, not at it.
- Finish most combinations with jabs to get back into correct on-guard position and minimize your vulnerabilities.
- When moving to get good position, stay close to your opponent so that you are still in range to score.
- Make all motions—punches and defensive movements—efficient.
- Practice to make your punches quick and well-timed so that you do not telegraph them.
- Never hesitate. If you throw a bad punch, continue with another punch, or move. Don't stop because you missed your target.

Your body will always resort to what comes naturally. Make perfection come naturally.

Making It All Come Together with Combinations

Defending against an opponent who throws one punch at a time is relatively easy. With a rest in between punches, you have time to prepare and plan to defend the oncoming attack. To be most effective in the ring, however, throw multiple punches. A set of multiple punches is called a combination. Because boxing has five fundamental punches—and since these punches can be thrown in any order and in any number—the list of possible combinations is considerable.

Combinations reflect different boxing styles and should incorporate punches with head movement and footwork. This is the ultimate goal of boxing: where offense becomes defense that, in turn, becomes offense (which becomes defense, and so on). Integrate defensive movement within your combinations, and finish a combination with defense in order to keep your opponent from immediately attacking you.

Combinations should flow, becoming rhythmic and easy: a cross, if thrown correctly, sets up a hook to the body or head, or the cross may also lead into a duck or a slide. If your combinations are jilted or awkward, then you are not using your momentum and balance to the fullest. Let the combination develop as you work it, blending defense and offense.

Also remember to vary the power behind the punches that comprise a combination. Not all punches in a combination should be soft or powerful. The tempo also may be varied within a combination. Changing speeds, power, and tempo within a combination can catch an opponent off-guard.

The following are classic combinations that have stood the test of time. Practice these, and experiment with variations on them. Then make some up on your own, and determine which ones work best for your style of boxing.

PRACTICE EXERCISES FOR COMBINATIONS:
1. Double or triple jab (1-1-1); moving forward or in either direction around the opponent.
2. Jab-jab to body (1-1b); quick advance.
3. Jab-pause-jab and cross (1-pause-1-2); slip or feint during the pause.
4. Jab-cross (1-2); quick advance, then circle to your left.

5. Jab-cross to body (1-2b); quick advance, then circle to the left.
6. Jab-jab-cross-jab (1-1-2-1); move to the right or left.
7. Jab-jab to body-cross to body (1-1b-2b); move to your left or right after combination.
8. Jab-cross-hook (1-2-3); duck or pivot out after combination.
9. Cross-hook (2-3); duck or pivot to move away from opponent.
10. Cross-hook to body (2-3b); circle to the left after punching.
11. Jab and hook (1-3); circle to right or left.
12. Jab-jab-cross-hook (1-1-2-3); circle to right or left.
13. Jab-hook-cross (1-3-2); forward, backward.
14. Hook-cross (3-2) or cross-hook (2-3); quick advance, then circling left or right.
15. Jab-uppercut-hook-cross-jab (1-4-3-2-1); advancing after the first jab.

**Keep your hands up.
Keep your body balanced.
Keep your mind focused.**

Chapter Two
Exercises and the Conditioning of the Boxer's Body

Practicing Technique Through Common Boxing Exercises

You can practice your boxing technique in a number of ways. Doing drills in front of a mirror, in the ring, and on various boxing bags provides opportunities for improving power, endurance, skills, and for learning new techniques. You will benefit most from workouts if you visualize imaginary opponents in front of you as you train. This will help keep you focused during drills and will prepare you to face actual opponents in the ring.

Mirrorwork

Working on form and shadowboxing in front of a mirror will reveal your technique from different points of view. You can correct your technique if you train yourself to watch critically in the mirror. Focus on everything: feet, legs, waist, shoulders, arms, hands, and head. Go through a mental checklist as you move, throw punches, and work defense. You may want to begin by moving in slow motion, then speed up your exercise as you train your eye to watch more quickly. Look for openings that an opponent would find if they were in front of you. Identify your weaknesses and correct them before an opponent takes advantage of them in the ring.

Shadowboxing

Shadowboxing with or without a mirror can also be used to sharpen technique. Every time you shadowbox you should focus on technique, visualize your opponent in front of you, and work up a sweat by covering much of the ring. Most people use shadowboxing to warm up and cool down, but neglect to use the exercise to improve their skills. Your workout should not include wasted exercises—don't just "go through the motions." Work to perform skills correctly, making every exercise work for you. Begin workouts with skill-building and review. Don't exercise simply to break a sweat.

Footwork

Footwork drills focus your attention on specific foot and body position. Take the opportunity to sharpen footwork every time you shadowbox and jump rope. Footwork also can be improved by working on defense against less experienced boxers—don't catch their punches; defend yourself by slipping/sliding, ducking, side stepping, and backpedaling. Finally, as shown in Figure 2.1, a rope tied at shoulder-level (approximately twenty feet long, tied diagonally through a ring) can provide an obstacle under which to duck while you advance forward and backward along the length of the rope. The side-to-side movement made in conjunction with the duck is called a u-dip, since the action resembles the letter "u".

Figure 2.1: Cross-the-ring rope duck while throwing punches.

Let the rope hit your shoulder to keep your movement tight and efficient; feel the rope graze the top of your head in order to avoid ducking too low. Once you are comfortable with this exercise, add punches as you move and duck to simulate competition.

Practicing Punches

Practice punching technique on bags, to strengthen your arms, sharpen your accuracy, and increase your speed, power, and stamina. Each bag has a different overall purpose. Punch bags the same way you would punch in competition. Move around the bags, hit them with varying intensities and speeds, and work both entire rounds and specific drills.

Working a round means that you hit the bag for an entire two- or three-minute round without rest. Working an entire round is difficult if you do it properly by throwing many punches and incorporating your defense. Since a bag does not hit back at you, you must imagine that it is hitting back. If you box a bag just like you would an opponent, you will increase your stamina, power, and skill.

Working drills involves burning out the shoulders and arms in order to increase your speed, power, and endurance. The list below outlines exercises for the heavy bag, double-end bag, speed bag, and maze ball.

Heavy bag

Double-end bag

Speed bag

Maze Ball

Focus mitts

Heavy Bag

The heavy bag is often mistaken for a bag that simply builds strength by providing resistance to punches. Though the heavy bag does build muscle and endurance, it should also be regarded as a tool for improving skill. Visualize the heavy bag as if it were an opponent—look for a head, stomach, and waist on the bag. Alter the speed and targets you hit for combinations that work upstairs (to the head) and downstairs (to the body), just like you would in a bout. Since the heavy bag doesn't move around, you have to move around it. Practice stepping around the bag to elude imaginary punches, and jab while constantly moving around to the right and left of the bag. Don't let the heavy bag swing too much—always try to hit it as it returns to you in order to provide the most resistance and to prevent the bag from swinging wildly.

EXERCISES FOR THE HEAVY BAG:

Work rounds in which you integrate offense with defense. Be sure to move each direction around the bag. You can also use the following drills:

Burnout drill: punch for speed at eye level, alternating the straight right and left punches. Begin with 5 seconds (followed by a 15-second rest), hitting the bag for a total of three minutes. Use short burnout segments to build speed, and longer segments to build endurance.

Power drill: punch for power at eye level, alternating the straight right and left punches. Start with 5 seconds (followed by a 15-second rest) for a total of 90 seconds. Try to work up to three minutes of power drills, alternating length of rest and work intervals.

Ladders: with the jab, punch the bag at eye level twelve times as quickly as possible—careful to maintain good form—then slip, slide, and duck. Next, punch the bag eleven times, then slip, slide, duck...step down all the way to one repetition. That's one ladder. Do ladders with both the jab and cross. Practice your defensive moves between ladder sets. Work up to three ladder sets with each hand.

Double-End Bag

Practicing speed and accuracy on a double-end bag can become a favorite workout. The elastic cords that anchor the double-end bag make it move fast, and therefore challenge your eye-hand coordination. It also forces you to punch and move your head quickly. Practice rapid-succession punching, combinations, and all defensive skills, including moving around the side of the bag. If you do it right, the double-end bag should be one of the most challenging and rewarding exercises you do.

EXERCISES FOR THE DOUBLE-END BAG:
For the double-end bag, work rounds using the following combinations that incorporate offense and defense:

1. double 1, slip
2. double 1, slide
3. double 1, 2, slip
4. double 1, 2, slide
5. 1, upper 1, slip, 2 hand
6. 1, long 3, u-dip
7. feint 1, short 2, duck
8. double 1, slip, short 2

Speed Bag

The speed bag can be used to sharpen technique, increase arm endurance, and improve eye-hand coordination. Hit the speed bag like you would strike any target. Punch the speed bag with each hand, alternate hands, and double-hit the bag sometimes. If the bag is moving too quickly for you, or if you want to increase the power necessary to move it, let out some of the air from the bag. Move around the bag as you strike it to increase the challenge and to remind yourself never to remain stationary. Practice the way you want to perform.

EXERCISES FOR THE SPEED BAG:
Work rounds. Use different techniques for each round, including some of the following techniques:

Single punches: alternate punches with each hand
Double punches: alternate double punches with each hand
Double punches with move: alternate double punches with each hand while stepping around to the right and then to the left side
Pin punches: pin the bag to the board using straight punches and upper cuts, alternating hands

Maze Ball

The maze ball can be used to practice defensive movements and punch timing. You never strike the maze ball with your fist: simply use a swinging maze ball to slip/slide/duck/u-dip/step/pivot around. Move purposefully around the maze ball; don't just get out of its way. Some people hang the maze ball in front of a mirror so they can keep an eye on the bag at all times, but it also can be used without a mirror. Place your body directly under the bag, and hang the bag high enough so you can duck without getting hit. Push the bag so that it swings in a straight line. Eventually you will develop a rhythm so you can work combinations of defensive moves without fearing the bag hitting you from behind. Once you become comfortable with the technique, start throwing combinations of punches within your defensive moves. The possible combinations are limitless.

EXERCISES FOR THE MAZE BALL:

For the maze ball, work rounds that incorporate the following combinations of offense and defense, such as:
1. slip, slide, or duck, then 1
2. duck, double 1 to the body
3. duck, 1, 2
4. 1, slip left, 1
5. 2, slip right, 2
6. slip left, 5, 4, duck
7. slip right, 4, 5, duck
8. slip right 2, 3, 2, duck
9. slip left 1, 2, 1, duck
10. slip left 3, 2, 1 or 3, 2, 3

Focus Mitts

Focus mitts, also known as punch pads, are a useful tool for working combinations and transitioning between offense and defense. The pads are worn on the hands of a workout partner, typically a coach, who holds the pads at differing angles as the boxer throws various punches. When holding the mitts for someone else, be sure to sometimes throw punches at the boxer so he/she can work on slipping, sliding, ducking, and

Figure 2.2: Hold focus mitts directly in front of the boxer to promote the throwing of straight punches.

catching. Also, hold punch pads directly in front of the boxer in order to encourage him/her to throw straight punches (Figure 2.2). When you hit focus mitts that someone else is holding, be sure to contact the middle of the mitt (usually marked with a dot) so you don't hurt the hand or wrist of your coach. Boxers also can benefit from holding focus mitts for a less-experienced boxer, since doing so can develop the skill of watching punches as they are thrown, thus sharpening the defensive eye.

Two other drills can help improve your punching technique, strength, and endurance:

Rubber band punches: with an elastic tube or band attached firmly to the ring post, throw a slow, straight punch while grasping the band (Figure 2.3). Gradually build up speed and resistance by increasing the speed at which you throw the punch. This is a good stretching exercise. As a burnout exercise, simply throw multiple punches for a maximum of one minute at a time. Alternate hands so that each arm gets work.

Figure 2.3: Rubber band punches.

Weighted punches: with a one-pound, two-pound, or five-pound weight, throw multiple punches at eye level. Punch like you're throwing a regular jab, then flip over the hand so that you are jabbing in an upward motion with your palm toward the ceiling like the upper jab (Figure 2.4). Repeat the flipping motion quickly with each jab. Work up to three sets of twenty repetitions on each arm.

Figure 2.4: Punches with small weight.

Sparring

Practicing skills with another boxer can be extremely useful. Working with a partner on specific skills by breaking them down into steps is called one-step sparring. Some one-step sparring drills are included in the essay

Exercises and the Conditioning of the Boxer's Body

entitled "Putting Your Skills to the Test: Sparring." When you work with other boxers, be sure to challenge each other and correct mistakes before they become habits.

Sparring is a chance to learn, exercise, and test your skills with another boxer. Think of your sparring partner as a partner, not as an opponent. Approach sparring as a controlled exercise, keeping in mind the skills you want to practice. Help make your sparring partners better—they will, in turn, challenge you to be a better boxer.

Working one-step sparring drills can be an effective method for learning specific skills.

Sparring should be done in moderation. Sparring is not the place to learn the fundamentals of boxing. Complete other exercises (jump rope, shadow box, hit bags) before you spar so that you are warmed up for sparring and you have burned off excess energy. Do not spar, however, if you are tired, because you will pick up bad habits such as carrying your hands low. You will benefit from sparring when your arms and legs are not at their absolute strongest, because this replicates what you will likely experience in competition.

Sparring hones your distance, footwork, and timing. Do not fight when you spar. Make yourself (and your sparring partner) stay under control and focused on the exercise. Use all your different punches, all your various defensive skills, and practice moving around your partner—don't just stand in front of him or her. You should not hit with all your strength; you should punch with approximately 60-80 percent of your power but with all your speed. Controlling punches will take some practice. Maintain your punching speed throughout the sparring session.

Visualization

Visualization is a proven means to improving technique. Visualize yourself throwing correct punches, gliding around the ring, evading opponents, and scoring punches. Imagine yourself doing everything with ease and not being tired. Imagine that you control the pace. Use visualization while resting, before you go to bed, while you run, jump rope, or shadow box.

Video can be a powerful tool, as well. Some athletes use video to capture bout or sparring performances. Running the tape in slow motion can reveal your strengths and weaknesses and improve your ability to visualize.

Finally, remember to practice perfectly. Your body always will resort to what comes naturally when it is tired, stressed, or hurt. Make yourself practice everything perfectly so that perfection comes to you easily in bouts. If you cheat in the gym, you will pay the price in the ring. Hard work now will pay off later.

Caring for Boxing Equipment

The number one cause of deterioration of boxing equipment is moisture. Be sure to dry your gloves, headgear, protectors, and handwraps after each use. A small fan or glove dryer used between workouts will keep your equipment dry and odor-free, since bacteria will be less likely to find a home.

The outside of gloves and other equipment should be cleaned with warm, soapy water. Avoid leaving equipment in direct sunlight, or in extremely hot conditions (such as in a vehicle). If gloves or other leather equipment are torn, they might be fixed at a shoe repair shop.

Your handwraps should be washed after every practice, especially if community gloves are worn. Clean, dry wraps will help absorb moisture and keep your boxing gloves odor-free.

In case gloves or headgear are exposed to blood, spray the affected area with a solution of ten percent household bleach to 90 percent water. This mixture is believed sufficient to kill any blood-born disease, such as hepatitis or HIV. Wash treated gloves with warm soapy water after you use the solution in order to minimize irritation bleach might cause to the eyes and nose.

Gloves and headgear should be checked regularly for tears and cracks. Repair or replace equipment according to manufacturer's specifications.

Safe practices require safe equipment.

Creating a Day's Workout

Each day's workout contains two components: cardiovascular training and a gym workout. If you are a beginner, or are out of shape, you should only participate in one training component each day. Those who wish to work cardio and skills on the same day should complete the aerobic exercise at a different time from the gym workout. If you do them separately, you will have enough energy to give your best effort in each training session. If running is not possible, be sure to include some other type of comparable aerobic training, such as jumping rope, bicycling, doing aerobics, etc.

While a good boxer must achieve cardiovascular fitness through regular exercise, gym workouts may be done as little as three times per week, and generally should last between one and two hours. In boxing, as in many sports, it is quality (not quantity) that develops skill. People who are in the gym too often (or for too long each training session) may develop lackadaisical training habits that will actually stunt or even reverse the progress they make in skill-building. If you are in the boxing gym only three times per week, but are focused on learning and performing skills to your utmost, you will benefit greatly from your workouts.

Though most coaches will provide a pre-planned workout, there will be times when you will have to develop your own gym workout. When creating a workout, consider the skills that you need to develop, and focus energy on mastering those techniques, while also including exercises that you enjoy. For example, beginners should include a majority of footwork drills, and only work on the punches that have been learned to date. Consider the level of difficulty of your workouts. Choose numbers of rounds for each exercise that will challenge you, and yet keep the intensity at a high level.

Variety in exercises and in the duration of exercises will not only develop the myriad skills needed in the ring, but will also help you keep your focus while training. Table 2.1 provides a list of the different types of boxing exercises. Complete four to six exercises for between one and four rounds each for every boxing workout. With so many exercises from which to choose, boxing workouts can vary greatly from day to day. Based on the list provided in Table 2.1, a sample workout is provided in Table 2.2.

Table 2.1
Exercises and Variations of Traditional Boxing Exercises

Jump Rope	as warm-up
	as aerobic training
Shadow Box	mirrorwork
	in the ring
Heavy Bag	combinations
	speed drill
	power drill
	ladders
Double-end Bag	combinations
	combinations with movement
Speed Bag	work through rounds
	pin drill
Maze Ball	evasive moves
	evasive moves with punches
Partner Exercises/Drills	focus mitts
	one-step sparring drills
	two-step sparring drills
	directed sparring
	open sparring

Table 2.2
Sample Daily Workout

Cardiovascular Workout	Running/Aerobics	>20 mins.
Gym Workout	Stretch/warm-up	5-10 mins.
	Jump rope	12 mins.
	Shadow box/footwork	4 rds.
	Heavy bag	3 rds.
	Speed drill (heavybag)	3 mins.
	Double-ended bag	3 rds.
	Maze ball	3 rds.
	Focus mitts with coach	3 rds.
	Shadow box	1 rd.
	Cool down/stretch	5-10 mins.

General Conditioning

Conditioning is achieved through aerobic training. Aerobic activities are defined as exercises that allow less than two seconds of rest for every 20 to 30 minutes of exercise. Boxers have regular rest intervals of one minute in bouts (and usually in practices), and though a boxer's oxygen supply is taxed for the two or three-minute work round, the rest bell allows the body to recover. Therefore boxing is technically considered an anaerobic activity. However, cardiovascular fitness is mandatory if you want to remain active during the entire bout.

Generally, for all aerobic activity, an athlete should remain in his/her heart rate's target zone (60 percent to 80 percent of aerobic capacity) for 20 to 30 minutes. Table 2.3 provides a general gauge of heart-rate goals. Measure your heart rate by taking your pulse immediately after you stop exercising. Count the beats while watching a clock. After six seconds pass on the clock, multiply that pulse count by ten to get your heart rate, then raise or lower your exercise intensity to meet your heart-rate goal.

Any aerobic activity should be preceded by about ten minutes of warming up, and the aerobic workout should always be followed by ten minutes of cooling down and stretching. Avoid straining your muscles by starting or finishing an aerobic workout too quickly without a proper warm-up and cool-down.

Boxing is a strenuous sport: first, your success in the ring depends solely on you; second, you have to remain active throughout the entire match. If you are tired, you cannot throw punches or move effectively in defense. You have a definite advantage if you are in better shape than your opponent.

In order to see positive results, you should exercise aerobically three and six times per week. Aerobic classes and videos of exercise programs such as step aerobics, boxercise, Tae-Bo, and others, typically elevate the heart rate for 25 to 45 minutes. Some other common

Table 2.3
Target Zones for Aerobic Activity

Age	Maximum Heart Rate	Warm-up Rate	Workout Rate
20	200	85	140-170
25	200	85	140-170
30	194	82	136-165
35	188	80	132-160
40	182	77	128-155
45	176	75	124-150
50	171	72	119-145
55	166	70	115-140
60	159	67	111-135

aerobic exercises include: bicycling, swimming, jumping rope, in-line skating and, of course, running.

Roadwork

Two different types of running, when used to complement each other, will give you a good result and an advantage in the ring: distance running and interval running. A complete roadwork program should include moderate distance and interval running, discussed at greater length in the essay entitled "Running Programs for Conditioning."

Jumping Rope

Jumping rope is an exercise that can improve footwork, arm strength, endurance, and coordination. It can also be an excellent way to warm up and cool down. Jumping rope for 20 to 30 minutes may be used as an aerobic activity for achieving cardiovascular fitness. These fundamentals of jumping will improve your efficiency:

Choose a good rope. The rope should be heavy enough to swing quickly. Leather, beaded, and plastic ropes work well. Some ropes have weighted handles to add to your arm workout.

Stretch front and back of legs and feet. Stretch your entire body before you jump, since jumping is a high-impact activity on muscles and joints. Hamstrings, quadriceps, calves, shins, knees and ankles should be warmed up before and after you jump rope.

Jump on a soft surface. A soft surface will reduce stress on your shins and also will require more energy than jumping on a hard surface. Jump in the ring or on a mat, if possible.

Take single jumps, don't skip. Your feet should jump once for every one or two rotations of the rope. Don't skip jump (taking a baby hop in between jumps). Bring the rope around quickly with your wrists so that the movement is fluid and you are able to develop a comfortable rhythm.

Take little jumps. Achieve little clearance over the rope. Doing so will help you speed up your jumping and will help you become better coordinated, since you can incorporate different types of movements.

Move your arms. Rotate your wrists slightly to flip the rope. Eventually you should learn to cross the rope in front of you and beside you in order to increase the arm workout. This skill takes some time to learn, so be patient.

Jump long enough. Try to work up to jumping between twelve and twenty-four minutes at a time. Take no rest breaks when you jump.

Exercises and the Conditioning of the Boxer's Body

Vary the intensity of your workout by incorporating different techniques, as well as different speeds.

Stay relaxed. Maintain steady breathing. Keep your chin somewhat tucked, and keep the muscles relaxed. Try not to get frustrated if you stop the rope often—everyone has bad days with the rope.

Maintain good posture. Keep your upper body aligned while jumping. The ears, shoulders, and hips should line up vertically.

Vary your jumping routine. When you are comfortable with the two-footed jump, vary your routine to include different types of jumps, such as the ones listed below.

VARIATIONS IN JUMPING ROPE:

1. Two feet together
2. One foot at a time
3. Knees up high
4. Feet kicked up in back
5. Double skip (two turns of the rope per jump)
6. Crossing arms in front of body
7. Backwards
8. Squat jumps (jumping in a "sitting" position)
9. Side to side (feet together)
10. Scissors (feet moving together, then apart)
11. Scissors (up and back with feet together)
12. Split jumps (one leg up while the other is back, alternating)
13. Twisting of lower body (feet together)
14. Rope over to each side of your body
15. Star figure (feet together, touch the points of an imaginary star on the ground)
16. Easy rock (with each turn of the rope, alternate your weight from from the right to left leg)
17. Boxer shuffle (kick the heel of one foot in front of your body as you land on the other foot, then jump with both feet together, and then alternate legs)

Resistance Training

Resistance training can improve strength and quickness in boxers. However, before you invest time and energy in a hard-core lifting routine, consider a general resistance program that involves different kinds of calisthenics as a way to strengthen muscles.

Calisthenics are a must for all good boxers. Push-ups, sit-ups, jumping jacks, mountain climbs, jump lunges, neck lifts, leg lifts, arm rotations, and stretching will make your body stronger.

Mountain climbs.

Later essays provide you with information about resistance-training exercises that can specifically benefit boxers. It is not necessary that you resistance train in order to box successfully; however, advanced boxers make resistance training a part of their overall workout since the benefits can be so great.

Some people think that wearing ankle weights around the gym or around the house will make them quicker once the weights are removed. However, if you practice with added weight on your legs, you will perform as if you have added weights on your legs, too. Your body doesn't know the difference between training and competing: if you have trained your muscles to respond slowly (because they are weighted down), then they always will—even in the ring. If you insist on using ankle weights, however, use them sparingly.

It is generally believed that if you use a heavy glove to work out, you will increase your speed when you box in lighter gloves. This is true, but only if you practice correctly. If 18-ounce gloves weigh you down so that you are not keeping your hands up properly or you find yourself punching slowly, then ditch those gloves—they are only reinforcing bad habits. If you plan to compete in 10-ounce gloves, then consider working out in 14-ounce gloves, again, provided you can work with them properly. If they are too heavy, then use a lighter glove. You can increase the glove weight when your strength and endurance improve.

Stretching and Warming Up

You will get out of boxing only what you put into it. If you are rushed with your workouts, then you should expect little return on your investment. If you neglect to stretch and warm up, then expect your body to get sore, tired, and injured. Many books and videos teach stretches for each of the muscle groups. The essay, "The Muscles Used for Boxing: Basic Stretches," provides some common stretches that can be used to protect and further develop range of motion. Boxing is a total body workout, so all muscles and joints should be warmed up before each workout.

The Importance of Rest

Rest is a vital part of any training program, as it allows sufficient time for the body to recover from workouts and/or tough competition. Resting is not a sign of weakness; it is a smart decision made by an educated athlete. To maximize your physical and mental energy, you should always allow recovery time:
1) between cardiovascular work and gym workouts, 2) between cardiovascular workouts, 3) between gym workouts, and
4) after competition.

Taking breaks after competition benefits you physically as well as mentally. If the competition was particularly taxing, or if you participated in a tournament in which you boxed for several days consecutively, then you should expect to take several days off from workouts in order to allow your body time to heal. If you have competed in a show or tournament that marks the end of your season (and you will not begin competing again for several months), you should take a break from the gym for several weeks. Taking time off guards against mental burnout. Continuing with cardiovascular workouts in the off-season will simplify your transition back into the gym. In addition, the break from the gym will make your return more enjoyable since your energy and interest will be renewed.

> **Smart training decisions lead to better boxing.**

Running Programs for Conditioning

Conditioning is the single most overlooked aspect of boxing training. Boxing matches cannot be won on heart or skill alone. However, when all other variables are equal—experience in the ring, skill level, size, and speed—the better-conditioned boxer has the advantage because he/she is able to throw more punches, stay under control, use more efficient defensive maneuvers, and keep control of the ring. Boxers in good condition can manage the footwork necessary to set up punches or turn defensive moves into offensive ones. Pushing the action, never letting up, and attempting to stay on the offensive are three elements to boxing that will frustrate your opponent and impress the referee and judges. To do these things you must be in good condition. Boxing has traditionally relied on running programs to achieve fitness.

The Secret to Roadwork

Coaches and boxers formerly believed that roadwork was best accomplished by steadily running long distances. Many boxers would jog slowly for as many rounds as their big fight was scheduled to last. It was thought that this style of roadwork improved endurance and helped the boxer lose weight. This training method, however, has proven to be an insufficient way to condition the boxer's body.

Research now indicates boxers need a running program that elevates the heart rate, and stretches and strengthens the muscles. While a slow jog can be good for loosening tense muscles, slow jogs do not challenge the muscles to fire as explosively as is needed in the ring. Your body will perform the way it has been practiced. If you practice moving slowly and steadily, then slow and steady is how you will perform in a match. If your goal, however, is weight loss or conditioning, a weekly running program which combines moderate distance with sprints (also called interval running) is best.

Running long distance promotes endurance because you are sustaining a pace over a long period of time. Distance runs for amateur boxing should be no shorter than 1.5 miles, but no longer than three miles at a time. If you reach a point at which you feel your distance run is not sufficiently challenging, increase your speed, or take a longer distance run once a week. Regular distance runs will provide a solid foundation on which to add sessions of interval running.

Running sets of sprints will improve endurance, recovery time, quickness, and explosiveness in the ring. Sprints (sometimes called "lifts") force air into your lungs and make your heart pump large amounts of blood to muscles that are forced to fire rapidly and recover quickly. Sprinting can take the form of straight sprints, running stairs, or sprinting hills. Always warm up and stretch properly before and after you run distance or sprints.

The tables, below, provide examples of interval workouts and distance workouts that you can use to create your own running program and schedule.

Table 2.4
Sample Workouts—Interval Days
Monday, Wednesday, Friday

Example 1:	jog for 8 minutes or 1 mile
	5 x 100-meter sprints (jog 100 meters to recover)
	8 x 50-meter sprints (jog 100 meters to recover)
Example 2:	jog 4 minutes or half a mile
	4 x round sprint–the usual round time of your bouts (jog until recovered)
	jog 8 minutes or 1 mile
Example 3:	jog 8 minutes
	3 x 1-minute sprints (jog until recovered)
	6 x 20-second sprints (jog back to starting line)
	jog 4 minutes
Example 4:	jog 800 meters
	8 x 200-meter sprints (under 30 secs.)
	jog 200 meters between sprints
	4 x 100-meter sprints (under 12 secs.)
	jog 100 meters between each sprint
	jog 400 meters

Table 2.5
Sample Workouts—Distance Days
Tuesday, Thursday, Saturday

Example 1:	jog half a mile
	run 2 miles in under 14 minutes
Example 2:	jog 4 minutes or half a mile
	run 1.5 miles in under 10.5 minutes
	jog 4 minutes or half a mile
Example 3:	jog 4 minutes or half a mile
	run 2.5 miles in under 18 minutes
Example 4:	jog one mile
	run 2 miles in under 14 minutes
Example 5:	run 3 miles at your own pace

Exercises and the Conditioning of the Boxer's Body

Walking lunges Fast-heel kicks Bounding for distance High skipping

Jumping in place while rotating the lower body Lateral shuffle Lateral crossover

Key Elements to Running Programs

There are a few important notes to remember when running for conditioning. First, make sure you continue to breathe while you are running/sprinting—don't hold your breath when you are really pushing yourself. Second, be sure to keep your chin level when you run (especially when you sprint): don't allow yourself to get into bad habits of lifting your chin or straining your face when you are tired. Third, maintain correct posture when sprinting: bring your knees up high and drive your arms to the sides of your body (not across your body). Finally, start your conditioning program slowly. As you get in better shape, shorten the rest time you take between sprints in order to increase your aerobic capacity. A quality running program can yield great results in the ring.

Running workouts should focus on four key elements: intensity (speed), volume (amount), frequency, and duration of your rest (recovery) interval. When you begin running for fitness, you will likely move rather slowly; however, as you continue with your program, you will be able to increase the intensity with which you run distance and sprints. The amount of running you do will also increase as you get in shape. Don't be discouraged if you can only run a short distance without stopping. With enough practice and patience you may eventually get to the point of being able to run several miles without feeling tired. The number of times you run each week will also increase as you become fit.

Again, always stretch adequately before and after any running workout, especially sprints. Dynamic warm-up exercises can be used to prepare the muscles for running sprints. On a flat surface, perform the following dynamic warm-up exercises for approximately 20 yards each: walking on the inside and outside of the feet, lunges walking forward, quickly kicking heels high behind you, high knees, bounding for distance, skipping while reaching high with each arm, running backwards, lower-body rotations, lateral shuffles moving backwards, and lateral crossover shuffles (facing both directions).

The body needs time to recuperate, and rest promotes muscle growth from the wear and tear of a challenging conditioning program. Take a rest from running every five to seven days. If you don't want to take an entire day off from your program, use your rest day to lightly jog two or three miles.

Effective cardiovascular training will benefit you greatly in the ring, allowing you to punch and move at will. Cardiovascular training is as important as learning offensive and defensive skills.

Right now your opponent is getting ready for you. Are you ready for your opponent?

Muscles Used for Boxing (Part I): Basic Stretches

Stretching is a vital part of every workout and competition. Stretching helps protect your body against injury, prepares your muscles and joints for working out, provides time to mentally focus on your task, and develops flexibility.

Static stretching is not sufficient to prepare your body before exercising or competing. Warm up your muscles by increasing your heart rate and by moving through the range of motions that you will be using in practice or competition. Jumping rope, shadowboxing, and hitting focus mitts can all be used to warm up. Finally, be sure to cool down your muscles after your workout or competition with shadowboxing or a slow jog. Static stretches can then follow the cool-down period to help prevent stiffness.

PHASES OF EVERY WORKOUT:
Stretch/Warm-up → Exercise → Cool-down/Stretch

Stretching all muscles will take about ten minutes, since you will hold each stretch for a minimum of twelve to twenty seconds. Think of warming up, moving through range-of-motion exercises, and stretching as an investment in your body's health.

Additionally, since all the joints of the body are taxed in boxing, be sure to prepare your joints for exercise by performing joint rotations during your warm-up phase. While jogging around the gym or stretching area, flex, extend, and rotate the fingers, wrists, elbows, shoulders, neck, waist, hips, knees, and ankles through their range-of-motion.

Stretch every muscle group. Use this illustrated list until you develop your own complete stretching routine. You will find that some stretches feel better to you than others, and you may also want to vary some of the stretches you find listed here.

NECK

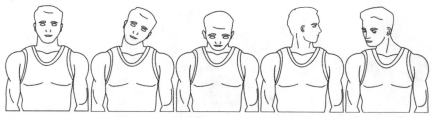

Flexion of neck over each ear, to each side, forward and diagonally

JAW

Exaggerated mouth movement

SHOULDERS, ARMS, CHEST AND HANDS

Shoulder pull on ring post or door frame   Triceps pullovers   Shoulder shrugs   Chest and shoulder pull-up   Arm across chest

Exercises and the Conditioning of the Boxer's Body

Pulldown against ring or table

Chest and arm against ring post or wall (Rotate the hand to stretch the biceps.)

Arms over head

Arm rotations

Shoulder rotations

Shoulder circles

Inside of forearm

Top of forearm

Exaggerated opening and closing of fists

Wrist rotations

STOMACH AND WAIST

Lateral lean-over (with or without weight)

Torso twists (seated or standing)

Cobra

BACK

Good mornings

Roll and arch the small of the back

Back bow

Knees to chest

Floor-torso twist

Seated-torso twist

HIP FLEXORS, KNEES AND ANKLES

Standing-hip flexors

Double-knee rotations

Ankle rotations

Exercises and the Conditioning of the Boxer's Body

QUADS, HAMSTRINGS AND GLUTS

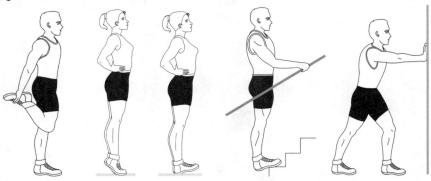

Standing quadriceps | Standing calf raises | Standing tibia raises | Heel off step | Front calf stretch

Shin stretch (lean forward on the front leg) | Toe touch | Crossed-feet toe touch | Hurdle stretch

Hurdle stretch using ring or table | Butterflies | Glut lean-over

Muscles Used for Boxing (Part II): Abdominal Muscles and Trunk Strength

The abdominal muscles are crucial for boxing movements, as they:
1. accelerate blows to the opponent;
2. promote slipping, sliding, and ducking (twisting the torso);
3. absorb blows to the body (tightening abdominal muscles reduces the effect of an opponent's punch); and
4. allow the legs and torso to move the entire body (and thereby evade punches entirely).

Sometimes the boxer who complains of sore ribs is actually experiencing soreness of the obliques that cover the small ribs. If you have not properly trained the oblique muscles, a tense bout or a tough workout can quickly cause discomfort that is easily mistaken for soreness caused by an opponent's blows. Strong abdominal muscles can make training easier, promote changes in body composition, improve self-image, and make punches and trunk movement faster and more efficient.

The abdominals work closely with the back muscles to turn the trunk for defensive moves and punching. The torso is divided into anterior muscles (in the front of your body) and posterior muscles (in the back of your body). Anteriorly, the abdominal region includes: rectus abdominous, transverse abdominous, and obliques (internal and external), or upper abs, lower abs, and obliques. Posteriorly, the lower back includes the erector spinae. If your lower back is fit, you also are likely to have good posture (and balance), and are less likely to develop lower back pain.

Stretch the abdominals before and after your abdominal training exercises. The cobra stretch and the knees-to-chest stretch are both good stretches for the trunk. Also use a static contraction of the abdominal muscles (tighten the muscles while you are standing) to increase muscle tone and prepare your muscles for activation.

For a complete abdominal workout, choose one or two exercises from each abdominal group to create a complete cycle of stomach exercises.

Cobra stretch   *Knees-to-chest stretch*

Exercises and the Conditioning of the Boxer's Body

The abdominals are resilient muscles and can be trained every day of the week. Note that a general boxing workout (which includes hitting bags, punch mitts, and/or sparring) will also increase the strength of the abdominals and back. If you train your abs every day, then vary the exercises you use from day to day, in order to maximize the result. When training, work your abdominals slowly, so all movements are controlled and focused only on the abs.

EXERCISES FOR UPPER ABS:
1. Crunches: curl up slowly (hands behind head or on legs, or outstretched overhead).
2. Tuck crunch: like a crunch, but with knees bent and feet off the ground.
3. Cross crunch: like a crunch, but with one leg crossing the other.
4. Crunch with legs up: like a regular crunch but with both legs extended straight upward (perpendicular to the floor).
5. Hover: laying on your stomach, flex the feet, bearing weight on your toes, lift yourself up onto your elbows. Use your abdominals to hover over the ground, keeping yourself in a straight position.
6. Bicycle: in crunch position, bring one knee up to the chest as you bring the shoulders off the ground, alternating legs and elbows.
7. V-ups: with arms parallel, stretched overhead, and legs outstretched, bring the hands and legs up overhead in a "v" shape.
8. Rope climb: in a modified sitting position, climb an imaginary rope with hands up, gently rocking the upper body to burn the stomach muscles—don't let your feet touch the floor.

EXERCISES FOR LOWER ABS:
1. Hanging knee-ups: let you body hang loose (by holding onto a chin-up bar, holding yourself up on elbows on an ab apparatus, or hanging by your arms in ab sleeves), slowly bring the knees up to your chest, then slowly lower your legs. For added exertion on the obliques, twist to one side when you bring up your knees.
2. Shooters: laying on your back, keep your legs straight up in the air with your feet together; slowly use your abdominal muscles to bring your pelvis only one inch off the ground.
3. Leg lifts: three to nine inches off the ground; move your legs in scissors, criss-cross, and circle patterns.
4. Knee-ins: with feet and knees together, keep your legs parallel to the floor, bring the knees into your chest, and return to original position.

The Ultimate Boxer

UPPER ABS

Traditional crunch

Tuck crunch
(legs bent in air or on bench)

Crunch with one leg crossed

Crunch with legs up

Hover

Bicycle

V-ups

V-up through legs

Rope climb

LOWER ABS

Bicycle

Hanging knee-ups

Shooters

Leg lifts

Scissors with leg lifts

Knee-ins

Exercises and the Conditioning of the Boxer's Body

5. Balanced knee-ins: sitting on a chair, a workout bench, or the floor, balance yourself with your feet off the ground. Bring your knees up to your chest and then straighten, repeat without letting the feet touch the floor.
6. Partner pushes: have your partner stand over your head as you bring your feet to their stomach (your legs remain straight); have them push your feet to the ground as you resist hitting the floor.
7. V-ups: bring your legs up and lift your torso up so your straightened arms extend beyond your legs.
8. Extension with wheel: supporting your body weight on your knees, slowly extend your body via the exercise wheel, then slowly bring yourself back into a kneeling position.

EXERCISES FOR OBLIQUES:

1. Side crunches: laying on your side, crunch upward.
2. Cross crunches: laying on your back, crunch up so your elbow almost touches the opposite knee (alternate elbow to knee).
3. Crunch with one leg up: keep one foot on the floor and other straight up in the air, curl up; switch legs.
4. Dumbbell side bends: hold a dumbbell (5 to 15 pounds) at your side, and move your torso sideways so the dumbbell moves down the side of your leg. Bring your torso back upright, and repeat.
5. Twists: stand with your feet shoulder width apart. Hold a broomstick behind your head and twist your torso to each side. Keep the movements controlled at all times—don't swing.
6. Lateral ball throw: throw medicine ball from side to side.
7. Bicycle: in crunch position, bring one knee up to the chest as you rotate the shoulders off the ground.
8. Balanced knee-ins with twist: bring knees to chest while balancing your weight on the floor or a bench, twist the opposite shoulder to knee.
9. Side jackknife: laying on your side, bring your torso off the ground as you raise your legs, with arms stretched overhead.
10. Partner pushes to the sides: same as partner pushes for lower abs, except your partner pushes your feet to each side of your body.

The abdominals are complemented by the muscles of the lower back. The following exercises can be performed at the same time you exercise your stomach. However, an intense back training routine

The Ultimate Boxer

Balanced knee-ins *Partner pushes* *Extension with wheel*

OBLIQUES

Side crunches *Crossover crunch* *Crunch with one leg up (bent or straight in the air)* *Crunch with knees to the side*

Lean-over *Trunk rotations (seated or standing)* *Lateral ball throw* *Bicycle*

Balanced knee-ins with twist

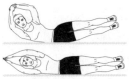

Side jackknife

Partner pushes to the sides

Exercises and the Conditioning of the Boxer's Body

should only be performed two or three times per week. Complete three sets of 8-15 repetitions for lower back exercises. Before you perform lower back exercises, stretch the back muscles using the seated back stretch, static floor back stretch, and/or the roll and arch.

LOWER-BACK EXERCISES:
1. Lean-over with (or without) weight: stand straight with knees slightly bent, lean to each side.
2. Good mornings: stand straight with knees slightly bent, lean forward bending only at the waist, then stand straight again.
3. Hyperextensions: on table or hyperextension apparatus with legs supported, lower the upper body by bending at the waist, then bring upper body parallel to floor. Keep your hands locked in front of you or behind your head. If more resistance is needed, hold a weight plate across your chest.
4. Superman hyperextensions: lie on your stomach with arms overhead. Lift your arms and legs by arching the lower back; hold for three to six seconds for each rep.
5. Dropped Superman leg lifts: with upper body supported on table or apron of boxing ring, slowly lower and raise the legs.
6. Seated row: keeping back straight and knees slightly bent, bring bar to chest. Focus on squeezing the shoulder blades together.
7. Trunk rotations: seated or standing, twist the upper body from side to side.
8. Standing lean-over with medicine ball: with light medicine ball extended overhead, slowly lean from side to side.
9. Seated-trunk rotations: while seated, with legs apart, move the medicine ball from side to side (bounce ball to each side).
10. Medicine ball throws: throw medicine ball from side to side. Throw ball either toward a wall or to a partner.
11. Punches with torso twist: with legs apart, punch from side to side, focusing on the lower back.

LOWER-BACK EXERCISES

Lateral lean-over with weight

Good mornings

Hyperextensions

Superman

Seated row

Dropped superman leg lifts

Trunk rotation (seated or standing)

Standing lean-over

Seated trunk rotation with medicine ball

Lateral ball throw

Punches to the side, twisting

Muscles Used for Boxing (Part III): Resistance Exercises that Improve Overall Strength

Boxing is a full-body exercise. It takes all muscles of the body to box well because you are throwing a variety of punches with both hands, slipping and sliding, ducking, moving forward, backward, to the right, to the left, and pivoting. Even if you are just standing still to throw a punch, you are using your legs, trunk, and arms to propel the punch. In fact, the arms are used very little compared to the trunk and legs. Physiology researchers found that a boxer's arms contribute only 24 percent to the punch, while the trunk and legs contribute 37 percent and 39 percent, respectively (Wallace and Flanagan, 13).

This list of strength-training exercises focuses on the muscles that aid the boxer in moving and throwing punches. These exercises should only be used once a baseline of fitness is achieved.

Overuse of muscles (over-training) will result in injury. The old adage: "No pain, no gain" is a myth. If you are actually working to the point of pain, then you may actually be harming your body. Push yourself in all of your exercises; however, listen to your body to know when you have worked it too much. Learn to push yourself without hurting yourself.

Always consult with a strength-training specialist to determine proper resistance and to be sure you are doing the exercises correctly. Most personal trainers will be happy to talk with you about your training program.

Although each major muscle group is mentioned here, stabilizer muscles are also included. Stabilizers are the smaller muscles that support major muscles. Stabilizers aid balance and help resist muscle injury.

If you are a beginner, or if you are pressed for time each week, place your focus on abdominals, back, neck, and wrist exercises. A sample Essential-Resistance-Training Workout is provided at the end of this essay. The remainder of this essay discusses all muscle groups, and provides lists of exercises from which to create a resistance training routine of your own.

Neck

The neck helps protect you from whiplash when you are hit. If your neck is not strong, you cannot properly keep your head up or move it to avoid being hit. When your neck is weak, little taps to the head from your opponent will appear as though you are getting hit hard (and getting hurt) because your head will snap back. The exercises below will focus on the posterior and side neck muscles. With all neck exercises and stretching, you should move slowly. Sudden or sharp movements could damage the spine and/or disks of the vertebrae. Do not hyperextend the neck (by pressing your head backwards) because that, too, can cause disk damage to the spine. Stretch the neck before strength training.

NECK EXERCISES:
1. Neck lifts: while laying on your back, bring your chin to your chest, then lower your head and repeat the exercise without allowing the head to touch the floor.
2. Look-overs: laying on your back, bring your head off the floor, look to the side, then up at the ceiling, look to the other side, and then back up at the ceiling. Do not touch your head to the floor between repetitions.
3. Side lifts: lay on your side, on one shoulder; let your neck drop down, then bring it up using the sides muscles of the neck only.
4. Wrestler's bridge: while lying on your back, bring your body off the floor by pressing down with your feet and your head. Roll onto your forehead and then to the back of your head to complete one repetition. This is an advanced exercise and should not be attempted until you have established a strong neck with other exercises.

The neck stabilizers, the upper fibers of the trapezius, are also important for overall neck strength.

NECK STABILIZER EXERCISES:
1. High pulls
2. Upright rows
3. Shoulder shrugs

Trunk

The trunk includes the abdominals and lower back muscles, and provides torque used to accelerate blows to the target, and evade punches thrown by the opponent. Exercises for the trunk muscles—the obliques (internal and external), rectus abdominous, transverse abdominous, and erector spinae—are provided in the previous essay. Review this essay to make sure abdominal muscles and lower back muscles are included in your resistance-training regimen.

Shoulders, Arms, and Chest

The shoulder propels the punch and also absorbs a lot of impact when your fist reaches its target. The entire shoulder must be toned, but the front (anterior) of the shoulder is most often taxed in boxing. Resistance training can help maintain shoulder balance so you don't suffer an injury because one portion of your shoulder is more developed than another.

All exercises done in the boxing gym should include some kind of shoulder stretching, since the shoulder is affected in all boxing drills and in competition. You can use a static stretch of the shoulder joint, but it is suggested that you also include some warm-up exercises that include a variety of shoulder movements.

Posterior lat pulldowns, posterior shoulder press and upright barbell rows should be avoided since they may aggravate or precipitate injuries to the shoulder. Arm stretches include: cross-body stretch, static shoulder stretch, arm rotations, and triceps stretch.

SHOULDER, ARM, AND CHEST EXERCISES (INCLUDING THE UPPER BACK):
1. Shoulder shrugs
2. Seated row
3. Bench press
4. Butterfly press
5. Front raises
6. Overhead press
7. Stiff-arm pulldowns
8. Push-ups (traditional or medicine ball)

SHOULDER STABILIZATION EXERCISES:
1. Push-ups on a medicine ball
2. Walkabout on medicine ball
3. Lateral raises

The arms (biceps and triceps) are integral to an effective punch. The arm extends the punch and quickly returns the fist to defensive position. While the arms are worked in most upper body exercises listed here, three specific exercises may also be used to develop arm muscles.

ARM EXERCISES:
1. Triceps dips
2. Triceps Press
3. Dumbbell curls

Hands and Wrists

Injury to hand, wrist, and upper extremities are the most common injuries among amateur boxers (Cordes, 1991). Breaking or stressing the small bones in the hand can be caused by improper technique or by contacting surfaces without proper padding on the hand. Additionally, injuries to the knuckles, wrist and arm are often caused by weak muscles, tendons, or ligaments.

The hands absorb a great deal of trauma even though they are wrapped and gloved. Any time you hit a bag, pad, or a person, you depend on the muscles and bones of the hand to hold up under a great deal of force. Likewise, the wrists are crucial since the wrists stabilize the fist (keeping it straight during punching and catching), and absorb a great deal of the punch that you deliver to your target. Skeletal injury to certain bones (such as the knuckles) is quite common among boxers, and fracturing a bone can keep you out of the ring for months while you fully recover. It is best to completely avoid injury to the bones, ligaments, or tendons of the hand by providing general conditioning as well as support with handwraps and gloves.

HAND EXERCISES:
1. Push-ups with a closed fist: contacting floor with the knuckles of the wrapped hand.

Exercises and the Conditioning of the Boxer's Body

NECK

Neck lifts   *Look-overs*   *Side lifts*   *Wrestler's bridge*

SHOULDERS, ARMS AND CHEST

Shoulder shrugs   *Seated row*   *Bench press*   *Butterfly press*

Front raises   *Overhead press*   *Lateral raises*

LEGS

Leg press   *Leg extensions*   *Leg curl*

The Ultimate Boxer

Calf raises (seated or standing)

Tibia raises

Mountain climbs

BACK

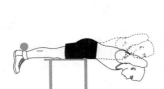
Hyperextensions

Good mornings

Anterior lat pulldowns

Seated row

Superman

Dropped Superman leg lifts

Trunk rotation (seated or standing)

2. Sand exercise: open and close your hand while it is submerged in a bucket of sand.
3. Hanging from chin-up bar: hold onto a chin-up bar for one-minute increments, and/or perform chin-ups or leg raises while hanging.

WRIST EXERCISES:
1. Wrist curls: palm facing up holding one to five pound dumbbell (high repetitions).
2. Reverse wrist curls: palm facing down holding one to five pound dumbbell (high repetitions).

Legs

You cannot be in good position to land a blow or move to evade an opponent's punches if your legs are not fit. Most of your leg endurance will come from cardiovascular (aerobic) training; however, leg strength is also important because it aids endurance and promotes explosiveness in the ring.

LEG EXERCISES:
1. Leg press
2. Leg extension
3. Leg curl

Hip Flexors

The hip flexors are used to pull your legs up and your stomach in. Curling your back in the boxer's stance, and moving your feet around the ring, engage the hip flexors. Generally, your hip flexors will be exercised with any activity that requires your knees to be pulled up toward your chest, such as jumping rope with high knees, sprinting, and leg lifts. However, if you are not doing these types of activities, the exercises listed below are recommended.

HIP FLEXOR EXERCISES:
1. Leg lifts: lift legs off the floor while lying on your back.
2. Knees-to-chest: lying on your back, or hanging, bring your knees into your chest, then back out straight.

Calves and Ankles

The calves are used to push your body around the ring. They are also isolated when jumping rope—a favorite boxing warm-up, cool-down, and aerobic exercise.

CALF EXERCISES:
1. Calf raises: seated or standing on a rise allows heels to move below the floor for maximum extension and stretch.
2. Tibia lifts: seated or standing.

Resistance Training Schedule

Experts now believe that effective resistance training can be achieved with two exercises per muscle group, two or three days per week. A typical resistance-training program might include a four-day-per-week routine, where arms are worked two days, and legs and back worked the other two days (thus each group works twice per week).

When you strength train you must continue your commitment to aerobic workouts. Resistance training is an anaerobic activity, and thus is not a substitute for cardiovascular training. Some weightlifters prefer to work their cardiovascular system before they lift, while others prefer to lift first, so they are stronger during their resistance training. It does not matter which you do first in a day. Be sure to stretch before and after resistance training, and even between sets of exercises, to promote flexibility and prevent injury.

Resistance training builds muscle: when you work resistance against isolated muscles, you must give the muscle time to rebuild itself by resting for a couple of days before working that muscle again. During the rest days muscle cells rejuvenate, producing a more toned muscle.

Following are two sample resistance-training schedules, based on a two-day per week exercise schedule. Notice the Total-Body Resistance Program will require lifting two or four days per week, working each muscle group twice per week. The Essential Program is for people just beginning to train, or for people on limited time budgets. They will work three days per week, but only specific muscles will be exercised. No weightlifting equipment is required for the Essential Program.

Exercises and the Conditioning of the Boxer's Body

ARMS

Traditional push-up

Push-up on medicine ball

Push-up with closed fist

Offset push-up on medicine or Swiss ball

Walkabout on medicine ball

Wrist curls

Reverse wrist curls

Triceps extensions

Triceps press

Triceps dips

Biceps curls

The sample schedules provide a break between neuromuscular groups, so your muscles have time to rebuild before you tear them down again with your next resistance training day. You can lift any day of the week, as long as you provide your body with an appropriate rest period between resistance workouts. The workout cycles below will take about 20 minutes (for the Essential Program) to one hour (for the Total Program). Note the repetitions are high with these workouts, since your goal as a boxer is not to bulk up, but to maximize strength and speed. High repetitions (12 to 15) and low weight will result in toned muscle.

When you lift, stretch or move through your range of motion while you wait to start your next set. You may even want to super-set some of your lifts. Super-setting is simply alternating between two different exercises for the completion of the sets. For example, you may alternate between lateral dumbbell lifts and wrist curls. While your shoulders recover from a set of lifts, you can work your forearms.

Table 2.6
Essential Resistance-Training Program
(3 days per week)

Exercise	Sets and Repetitions
Upper Abdominals	1-3 sets x 25 to 50 repetitions
Lower Abdominals	1-3 sets x 25 to 50 repetitions
Obliques	1-3 sets x 25 to 50 repetitions
Supermans	1-3 sets x 12 to 15 repetitions
Good Mornings	1-3 sets x 12 to 15 repetitions
Neck Lifts	1-3 sets x 12 to 15 repetitions
Neck Side Lifts	1-3 sets x 12 to 15 repetitions
Neck Turns	1-3 sets x 12 to 15 repetitions
Wrist Curls	1-3 sets x 12 to 15 repetitions
Reverse Wrist Curls	1-3 sets x 12 to 15 repetitions
Sand Exercise	1-3 sets x 12 to 20 repetitions
Tricep Dips	1-3 sets x 12 to 15 repetitions
Push-ups	1-3 sets x 12 to 30 repetitions

Exercises and the Conditioning of the Boxer's Body

While the forearms are recovering you can work the shoulders. Supersetting greatly reduces your recovery intervals, which means your workout will move along faster. Finally, since resistance training will initially make you sore, you should not begin a resistance training routine within three weeks of a major competition.

Any resistance-training program requires you to choose between a variety of exercises. The Total-Body Resistance Training Program lists examples of possible exercises for the various muscle groups. Use this program only if you are already fit and after you have completed several weeks of the Essential Resistance-Training Program. Consult a weight-training specialist to ensure your weight-training program is modified for you, and that you are doing each of the exercises correctly and with the proper resistance.

Table 2.7
Example of Total-Body Resistance Training Program (Four Day Split Program)

Upper Body: Monday and Thursday	Lower Body: Tuesday and Friday
Inclined Bench Press	Back Extension
Seated Butterfly	Seated Row
Anterior Lat Pulldowns	Bicep Curls
Over the Head Press	Tricep Extensions or Dips
Dumbbell Lateral Raises	Leg Press
Wrist Curls	Leg Extensions
Reverse Wrist Curls	Leg Curls
Walk-overs	Calf Raises
Neck Lifts	Tibia Raises
Neck Side Lifts	Crunch with Legs Up
Neck Side Turns	Leg Lifts
Traditional Crunches	Balanced Knee-ins with Twist
Abdominal Shooters	Hanging Leg Raises
Side Crunches	Sand Exercise for Hands

Increasing Your Power with Plyometric Training

Power is the combination of strength and speed. In a boxing match, power is evident in explosive punches and movements. European scientists devised a workout program that created the kind of explosiveness that all coaches wanted to develop in their athletes. They called it "jump training." Today, this jump training (now called "plyometric training," since it also involves exercises for the upper body) is widely used around the world in virtually every sport.

Plyometric exercises force specific muscles to reach their maximum strength in a short amount of time, thereby increasing the muscles' overall power. When punching a target, boxers contract their muscles in two ways: concentric contractions (shortening the muscles that accelerate the arm forward and back) and eccentric contractions (lengthening the muscles under the tension of making contact with the target). Boxers should work on both kinds of muscle contraction, thereby developing a quickness that incorporates speed with strength.

To increase speed/quickness, the eccentric contraction must immediately be followed by the concentric contraction. Hand and foot speed will increase as you learn the skills of boxing. However, once these skills are developed you can further increase your power with plyometric exercises for upper and lower body.

For maximum results, incorporate a plyometric program into your current training program about six to eight weeks before the date you desire to peak. Plyometrics should only be used one or two times per week because these exercises place a lot of stress on the joints. Give your body time to recover between workouts (similar to what you must do for resistance workouts).

Plyometrics are anaerobic, and thus may not be substituted for aerobic activity. Further, if you do not take sufficient breaks between reps and sets, then you will not maximize the power conditioning of the exercises.

Do not participate in a plyometric program if you are out of shape. Since leg plyometrics are high impact on the joints, do not participate in bounding and jumping if you are obese. Take caution if

Exercises and the Conditioning of the Boxer's Body

you are a heavyweight or super heavyweight, even if you are in good shape. As with other exercises, consult your healthcare provider before participating in a plyometric program.

Since you are overloading the muscles, stretch muscles before and after your plyometric exercises. Use dynamic warm-up exercises to prepare the muscles for the specific drills. Finally, assess your power levels before and after your program so you can measure your progress.

Evaluate your baseline power level:

How many push-ups can you do in 30 seconds? _____

How many sit-ups can you do in 30 seconds? _____

How far can you throw the medicine ball using an over-the-head toss? _____

How far can you throw the medicine ball using a one-handed chest pass? _____

REMINDERS FOR PLYOMETRIC TRAINING:
- Plyometrics should be used only one or two times per week.
- Begin your plyometric program about six to eight weeks before you want your power to peak.
- Consult an exercise specialist before you begin plyometrics so your program can be tailored to meet your specific needs.
- Warm up properly before your plyometric workout.
- Always do leg plyometrics on a soft surface since these exercises put excessive stress on the joints.
- Perform all plyometric exercises explosively: make your body move, push, pull, throw, or jump as powerfully as possible.

Arm and Trunk Plyometrics

Arm and trunk plyometrics involve the upper body in pushing, pulling, throwing, or twisting motions. The forceful and rapid movements that plyometrics require of the arms and trunk will help you punch more quickly and with greater force in the ring, thus helping you to punch more powerfully.

Many plyometrics incorporate the use of a medicine ball. When using a medicine ball, choose a weight between four and fifteen pounds, depending on your strength level. You can also choose between a variety of materials that cover the ball: leather, canvas, nylon, vinyl, and rubber. Most arm plyometric exercises that incorporate a medicine ball assume that you have a workout partner with whom to throw the ball back and forth. Use a rubber medicine ball to throw against a wall if you don't have a partner.

Be sure to stretch and warm up the arms and trunk before you participate in a plyometric program. At a minimum, you should warm up the arms and trunk with joint rotations such as jumping jacks, arm rotations, and trunk twists. Practice the motions of each exercise you will perform before you attempt it at full speed, to make sure you are properly warmed up.

The list below provides examples of plyometric exercises for the upper body. Choose among these exercises for use in your own plyometric program. For best results, do six to ten repetitions for three sets of each exercise you choose.

Power = strength + speed

Exercises and the Conditioning of the Boxer's Body

Push-ups:
Traditional push-ups with arms shoulder-width apart.

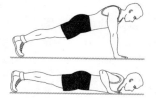

Close grip push-ups:
Traditional push-ups with both hands close together or on the medicine ball.

Offset push-ups (each side):
Traditional push-ups, however one hand stays on the medicine ball.

Underhand throws:
Keep your back straight, bend legs to pick up the medicine ball in front of you, raise straight up and throw the ball up and out to the target (focus on using your legs).

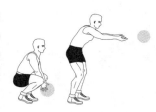

Power drops:
Lie on your back with arms stretched upward so you catch the ball being released by your partner. Once you've caught the ball, immediately throw it back up to your partner using a chest pass.

Lateral throws:

Stand with feet shoulder-width apart, with one shoulder facing your target (so you are sideways). Toss the ball with both hands, focusing on using the waist to propel your toss.

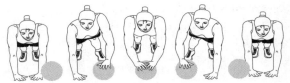

Seconds of walkabout:

With your outstretched arms, walk your body from one side of the ball, to the other. Move back and forth for 30 seconds.

Standing lean-overs:

With the medicine ball overhead, lean to the right and then to the left. Focus on the obliques and lower back.

Trunk rotation (each side):

Sit on the floor with legs apart. Rotate to one side and place the medicine ball behind you, turn to the other side to pick up the ball. Repeat the process. The ball will travel in a complete circle.

Standing-trunk rotation (each side):

Standing back-to-back with your partner, rotate to one side to pass the medicine ball back and forth between the two of you.

Over-and-under pass:

Standing back-to-back with your partner, pass the medicine ball to each other over your heads and between your legs. Switch half way through so that you are handling the ball in each direction.

Sit-up toss:

In the sit-up position, throw the medicine ball to your partner as you come up, then your partner tosses (or hands) you the ball on your way back down.

Sit-up toss with rotation:

Same as the sit-up toss, but twist and bounce the ball to each side of your body before throwing it back to your partner.

Overhead throws:

Stand with the medicine ball over your head (arms extended straight), and throw the ball while stepping forward with either leg as you throw. Pass the ball to a partner, or use a rubber medicine ball to throw to a wall.

Overhead throwdown:

Stand with the rubber medicine ball over your head (arms extended straight), and throw the ball to the ground in front of you. Bounce the ball to a partner or wall. Focus on using the lower back and arms.

Chest pass:

Standing straight, bring the medicine ball to chest level and push the ball toward the target with both hands. Step forward with one leg as you throw.

One-handed chest pass:

Same as above, but only using one arm at a time (similar to how you would throw a punch). Step forward with one leg as you throw.

Leg Plyometrics

Leg plyometrics engage the muscles of the legs and gluts in a variety of running and jumping exercises, such as jumping in place, hopping, bounding, jumping on and/or off of boxes, and running up steps. These exercises will help develop explosiveness with the legs, which can translate into faster movements in the ring, such as moving toward or away from the opponent, or using the legs to develop power for the punch. Though boxers do not need to specifically increase their vertical jump, bounding exercises also improve acceleration, change of direction, and push-off speed.

Warm-up for leg plyometrics should be done on a relatively soft surface like wood, grass, or on a track. Each of the suggested dynamic warm-up activities should be performed over distances of about 20 yards. Your goal in the warm-up phase is to increase your body temperature, blood flow, and prepare your muscles for intense training. These exercises will also improve your overall coordination. Warm up doing, at a minimum, the following exercises:

- Jogging
- Skipping (bringing alternate knee up to waist level)
- Marching (walking with high knees)
- High knees
- Walk lunges
- Backward running

The list below provides several examples of plyometric exercises for the legs. Choose a few of these exercises for use in your own plyometric program. For best results, do six to ten repetitions for three sets of each exercise you choose.

Agility change-of-direction hops:

Imagine yourself standing in the middle of a clock on the floor. Make marks at 12 o'clock, 2, 4, 6, 8, and 10 o'clock about 24" from the center. Starting in the center, jump with both feet to the 12 mark, then jump back to center, then jump to the 2 mark, then jump back to center, and continue with the rest of the marks until you are back where you started.

Agility lateral hop:
Mark a line on the floor and jump quickly from one side of the line to the other. Keep your feet low to the ground. Focus on your speed.

Agility single-leg lateral hop:
Same as above, but only one leg at a time.

Agility forward-and-backward hop:
Mark a line on the floor and jump quickly in front of and behind the line. Keep your feet low to the ground. Focus on speed. This drill can also be performed with one foot at a time.

Agility four-corners hops:
Same as above, but jumping diagonally between four corners of a square on the floor.

Tuck jump:

Standing on a soft surface, jump straight up so your knees are high in front of your body. Focus on quick explosive jumps high off the ground.

Tuck jump over hurdles:

Perform the tuck jump over several hurdles or foam barriers. Jump up and forward to clear the barrier.

Depth jump with double-leg bound:

Standing on a 12" or 24" box, drop to the floor landing on both feet, then jump quickly upward.

Double-leg jumps to 12" or 24" box:

Stand facing the box with feet shoulder width apart (to add difficulty, place your hands behind your head), and jump up to the box. Step back down and repeat.

Lateral step-ups to 6" or 12" box:

Stand to the side of a box, and step onto the box with the foot closest to the box. Use the leg nearest the box to bring your body up until the leg on the box is extended. Lower yourself back down to the ground, then repeat. Don't use the foot that is on the ground to push off; use the leg on the box to bring yourself up.

Double-leg bounding (stadium hops):

Bound up large steps with both feet (advanced boxers should place their hands behind their head). Keep legs bent.

Alternate-leg hop onto box:

With one leg on the box or step, jump upward and switch the position of your legs in the air so that you land with the opposite foot on the box. Continue alternating feet.

Fast feet on small steps:

Run quickly up small steps. Keep legs bent and feet moving as quickly as possible.

Single-leg hop-up:

Using one foot at a time, hop up small steps. Keep the leg bent.

Alternate-leg hop-up:

Alternating legs, jump up small steps laterally. Keep the leg bent.

Stadium circuits:

In a stadium or arena, jog to each set of stairs where you alternate exercises such as fast feet, alternate-leg bounding, double-leg bounding, and lateral stepping (alternate halfway up).

Forward cone hops (double or single-leg):

Stand facing a line of cones (about 4 to 8 cones, depending on your ability), and hop forward over each one. Use both arms to propel yourself up and forward over each cone. Try to minimize the time you spend on the ground between each of the cones.

Lateral cone hops (double or single-leg):

Stand sideways to a line of cones (about 4 to 8 cones, depending on your ability), and hop sideways over the cones.

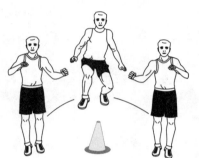

Alternate-leg bounding:

Exaggerate a run using leg and arm movements so you cover more ground with your legs than typically when running. Try to cover as much ground as possible by using the arms to pull yourself up and forward. When done correctly, you will seem to hover in the air.

Bounding with double-arm action:

Same as previous, but move arms together to propel yourself up and forward.

Jump and run:

Place two cones approximately 18 feet apart. Jump over one cone, turn to your right and run to the next cone, turn to your right to jump over that cone. Immediately after landing, turn to your right and repeat the process.

Chapter Three
The Science of Boxing

Secrets to Success (Part I): Winning Bouts

All boxing works on a point system. In amateur boxing points are awarded when boxers land a "clean blow." A clean blow (also known as a "scoring blow") meets five criteria:

1. It must land directly with the knuckle part of the closed glove of either hand.
2. It must land on any part of the front or sides of the head or body above the beltline of the opponent.
3. It must have the weight of the body or shoulder behind it.
4. It cannot be blocked/guarded by the opponent.
5. It may not be thrown while infringing on a rule.

This five-part criteria is the only way to score in amateur boxing. Because most boxers do not understand this, they win or lose very close decisions without knowing how to improve their skill level. Uneducated boxers are doomed to repeat the same mistakes over and over. However, if you understand these rules and keep them in mind when you train, spar, and box competitively, you will maximize your winning potential.

To use this knowledge to your advantage, you should understand the technical aspects of each of the above criteria for scoring blows. The following points explain the criteria and provide useful reminders for training and mentally preparing for competition.

1. Scoring blows must connect with the knuckle part of the closed glove. You may only touch your opponent with the knuckles of your fist. Some gloves mark the knuckles with a white patch, but most of the time you (and officials) have to use your best judgment. The most common is making contact with the inside of the fist, or palm (a slap). Correctly connecting with your target will "feel right" as the knuckles "dig" downward and inward, but you have to practice this correct punch in order to depend on it in bouts. If you hear a loud "thud" when you make contact with heavy bags or your opponent's body or head, you have likely not thrown a correct punch. Referees listen for this sound, and will take it as a signal that you are hitting with the palm of your hand.

2. The punch must land in a legal scoring area. The only legal scoring area is the front or sides of the head or body above the beltline of your opponent. You will not score a point if you hit your opponent

in the back of the head, below the belt, or on their back.

3. Punches will score only if they have the weight of the body or shoulder behind them. In order to throw and land an effective shot, you must extend your arms and move your body accordingly. Oftentimes boxers who have their opponents on the ropes or in a corner think they can rack up points by throwing lots of little shots to their opponent's head and/or body. Instead this practice just wastes energy, since rapid-fire punches do not meet the scoring-blow criteria.

4. Punches will not be counted as scoring blows if they are blocked/guarded by the opponent. This part of the criteria seems obvious, but most novice boxers don't understand the importance of making contact where their opponent is not blocking or guarding. It is important information for two reasons: 1) you are wasting energy if you hit an opponent when the shot will not count as a scoring blow, and 2) you leave yourself open to be countered every time you land a punch that is blocked. Landing punches to the arms and gloves of your opponent may look impressive to your friends and family, but it will not impress the judges, referee, your coach, or fans who really understand the sport. Take time when punching to see the openings. Sometimes you have to make openings happen if your opponent covers well. Make openings by varying your punches, punch placement, and the intensity and speed of the punches.

5. Judges will not count a punch as a scoring blow if you land the punch while you are infringing on a rule. If you hold with one arm while punching well with the other, it will not count as a scoring blow because you were holding. If an illegal punch hurts the other boxer so he/she cannot continue, you will lose the bout because you infringed on a rule.

In summary, with the scoring blow rule, the International Amateur Boxing Association (the organization that governs amateur boxing internationally) is making a commitment to the quality of boxing around the world. You must punch accurately, effectively, and with style. By keeping these scoring blow criteria in mind you will increase your skill and improve your chances of winning amateur bouts.

> **To be a champion, act like one.**

What if I am evenly matched with my opponent?

In cases in which scoring blows are equal between boxers, amateur boxing judges are instructed to score the winner based on his/her mastery of the ring, called "ring generalship." Ring generalship is based on three criteria observed by judges, as explained in the USA Boxing: Official Rulebook 1998-1999:

1. "Who has done most of the leading off or was the aggressor?"

Be first in your bouts. Even if you prefer to counterpunch, don't always wait for your opponent to lead. This is not to say you must always punch first. Certainly you should counter sometimes. Starting the action shows you are interested in the competition and eager to box: it also shows you have control of the ring and the action. You may wish to lead with a jab, a side step, or even a feint.

You have many opportunities to "be first." At the first bell, after the referee stops and starts the action, and/or after the referee calls for a break in the action. Attempting to punch or feint first indicates to the judges your desire to engage the other boxer.

2. "Who has shown the better defense (blocking, parrying, ducking, side stepping, etc.) by which the opponent's attacks were made to miss?"

Use defense and offense together. Do not always move straight forward and attack your opponent. Be smart and box with style. Show the judges that you are better skilled because you can defend yourself with defense as well as with offense. Capitalizing on your opponent's mistakes (by parrying sloppy jabs, for example) shows that you have command of your opponent.

3. "Who boxed cleaner and had a better style?"

Using fouls to your advantage will hurt you in the long run, and it is not a fair way to box. Boxing "clean" means you do not foul, or if you do foul, you correct the problem and do not repeat the same infraction. Similarly, a better style means that you box clean, and that you showcase a wide variety of punches and defense.

If you score the greater number of clean blows and establish ring generalship, you will be the superior boxer. The only way to achieve your maximum skill level in bouts is to demand perfection of yourself every time you work a heavy bag, double-end bag, speed bag, focus mitts, and when you practice footwork, shadow box, and spar with teammates.

Secrets to Success (Part II): Taking Advantage of Things Other Boxers Don't Do

Below are three pieces of advice offered to volunteer referees at USA Boxing, Inc., as outlined in the 1998 edition of its rulebook. You can use this information to your advantage by applying these tips to your boxing strategy.

1. [Concerning good referee positioning, note that] "Most [right-handed] boxers move in a clockwise manner in the ring. They occasionally move counter-clockwise; however, that is somewhat infrequent."

Basically, if most right-handers move to their left (usually in a pivoting fashion) you (if right-handed) should sometimes move to your right. Doing so will surprise your opponents, by making it less natural for them to move. Additionally, moving to your right will keep you out of the path of a right-hander's power punch. You will also be better prepared for left-handed boxers who like to move counter-clockwise. Moving against the grain is a skill. You must practice it frequently before it feels natural in a bout. Change up your movements. Make your opponent look for you. Don't get in a habit that your opponent can identify as a pattern.

Referees are instructed to identify the stronger boxer, and move off of his or her lead. If you are controlling the direction of movement, the referee will correspond, and the judges will instinctually pick up on this. You will also (noticeably) make your opponent look bad if he or she is moving in a direction that is uncomfortable—and judges will take this as a sign that you have the superior style.

2. "The first and most important duty of the referee in amateur boxing is to prevent either boxer from receiving unnecessary and excessive blows. The referee must immediately stop the boxing when a boxer appears unable to properly defend himself/herself."

Stay out of the corners and off the ropes where you may appear to have lost control of the bout. If you are covering up, even if you are not being hit with clean blows every time, the referee may think you are being passive, and he or she will stop the bout in order to protect you.

Some boxers make the mistake of playing the "rope-a-dope" trick made famous by Muhammed Ali, in which he would let his opponents hit him for a long time so that they would become tired; then he would return the attack. The risk of using this srategy is twofold: it is dangerous to your health; and the referee may stop the bout believing you can no longer protect yourself.

Don't give the referee an opportunity to stop the bout because you are waiting for an opening. Sometimes you have to create openings by feinting, punching your way out, and/or by moving out of the corner via a duck and pivot (or side step). Judges often believe that boxers who control the middle of the ring are the ones in charge. Though this may not always be true, you might use this as an aspect of your ring generalship. Control the pace and the space.

3. "The referee is there to see that the rules are followed...[they] have the responsibility to interpret the rules of the contest for which [they] are officiating and to decide any question not provided in the rules."

This directive means two things for boxers. First, don't foul. If you are called for a foul—even if you don't think you really committed it—then don't repeat it. Referees have the power to take a point away from you when you foul. But more importantly, the referees and judges (and fans) will start judging you as a boxer who fouls. Second, don't argue with the referee or judges. They have difficult jobs, and they are doing them to the best of their ability. Showcase good character by taking everything in stride: you don't always have to agree with officials, but show them the respect they deserve.

You will notice that the officials improve as your skill and style improve. This has less to do with the officials than it does your attitude and ability. If you are much better than your opponent, the referee and judges will not have to depend much on subjectivity. Make their job easy by being, without question, the better boxer.

An educated boxer wins more bouts than a boxer who doesn't understand the fundamental principles of boxing.

Secrets to Success (Part III): Character Counts

Winning bouts requires both physical and mental preparedness. Successful amateur boxing depends on your ability to showcase your talent in competition. Below are several fundamental principles to keep in mind when you enter the ring.

Box with style. Style refers to the special talent that you bring to the bout. Style includes impressive skill (offense and defense), finesse, and "clean" boxing. Style does not include hot-dogging. Although hot-doggers get a lot of attention in sports like football and baseball, people (especially boxing judges) believe boxers who show off are disrespecting their opponents. If you happen to be considerably better than him/her, don't rub it in by dancing around, lowering your guard, sticking out your chin, turning your head to the side, or taking wild looping shots. Beat your opponent with skill, not with silly or distracting antics. If you truly outmatch your opponent, the referee will recognize this and will stop the bout.

Win graciously. After every bout you should shake hands with your opponent. Thank your opponent's corner, and thank the referee. Be respectful to your opponent, his/her coaches, the officials, and fans. Don't flaunt the win in your opponent's face. Show everyone you are a boxer of character.

Lose graciously. There is nothing wrong with losing. The best boxers in the world have lost bouts. The key to losing graciously is accepting the fact that someone outboxed you...this time. You can always come back. Stay positive and contemplate the moment—use your loss to improve your skill level. Ask coaches what you did wrong, watch the video tape, work on the skills that got you in trouble. There is nothing wrong with being disappointed in your performance. Many variables are involved in winning and losing; accept that without making excuses. Your character will not be measured by how many wins and losses you have, but by how you react to those wins and losses.

Recognize that you are only part of the event. All officials in amateur boxing are volunteers. This includes referees, judges, timekeepers, clerks, weighmasters, announcers, computer technicians, inspectors, the jury, and physicians. All of these officials are registered and certified through their national governing body, which means that they have paid dues and completed a certification process (including workshops and tests). All of this training goes unpaid. Officials are motivated to help with amateur boxing programs because they like the sport and its athletes. Respect the official's time, energy, and love of this sport by being courteous at boxing functions. You may want to recognize officials by smiling as you pass by, by greeting or engaging them in conversation, or by going out of your way to thank officials for their hard work.

Many boxers follow a short formula at the end of a bout in order to show appreciation for their opponent and officials: 1) thank your opponent by touching gloves, hugging, or telling him/her that he/she boxed well; 2) thank your opponent's corner (coach) by touching your glove to his/her hand; and 3) thank the referee when you come to the center of the ring as you wait for the result to be announced. Some boxers also give a quick bow to each of the four sides of the ring where judges sit. People will remember your good character if you are courteous both inside and outside of the ring.

Self-discipline in the ring brings success. It reflects your committment to the sport and your willingness to uphold the highest standards of boxing.

> **Boxing isn't about fighting.**
> **Boxing is about boxing.**

Reading Your Opponent's Style

A smart boxer is difficult to beat. But being smart in the ring is more than just knowing techniques. You must know what strategies will work best in competition. Not all strategies will work against all boxers. To be successful in competition, you must learn to read your opponent.

Reading someone's boxing style is like reading a book. You cannot know the contents of a book by skimming over the first few pages. And you cannot accurately read a boxer's style simply by watching him or her for a few seconds at the beginning of the first round of your bout. Reading a style takes time, but this investment can turn your opponent's weaknesses to your advantage. Reading a style takes practice. It is a skill that can be used to help your teammates, or to dismantle your opponent's strategy.

Watch for these patterns when gauging someone's style of boxing:
1. Do they prefer to back up or move forward when they box?
2. Do they rush forward, or stay controlled?
3. Do they start the sequence, or prefer to counterpunch?
4. Do they always lead with the same hand?
5. How many punches do they throw in a typical combination? How do they react after they finish their combinations?
6. How, and in which directions, do they move? Do they move during an offensive attack? After combinations? Only on defense?
7. Do they drop one hand when throwing the other?
8. Do they over-extend on their punches?
9. Is their jab lazy?
10. Do they throw any feints?
11. Are there clues that they are going to throw a specific punch? What punches, if any, do they telegraph?
12. What is their pace? Do they tire at the end of the round? Are they slow in the middle? Do they end rounds in a flurry?
13. What distance do they typically maintain from their opponent?
14. Are they often caught on the ropes?
15. What punches would be effective against their attack?
16. How is their endurance? At what point do they get tired?

When you can answer questions like these about any potential opponent, then you have valuable information to use against them, and you have developed an observant eye. You can begin to plan how to capitalize on your opponent's habits and mistakes.

EXERCISES TO IMPROVE OBSERVATION:

1. Hold punch pads for inexperienced boxers. Work on simple techniques such as throwing the jab, the cross, slipping and ducking. While you hold the pads, watch your student's form. Correct his/her form, and show some of the consequences of poor form.
2. Work a defensive round against a less experienced boxer. Allow him/her to throw punches at you, and only throw a jab back if he/she does something wrong (e.g., their hands drop on the attack). Make your teammate miss. For example, as soon as your teammate becomes set to punch, you move. You can also improve your own defense by staying in the boxing zone some of the time, forcing yourself to use catches, slips, and side steps.
3. Watch boxers who are better than or equally matched with you while they are sparring or doing one-step sparring drills. Look for habits they have formed in the way they move, the punches they throw (variety, sequence, or number), or in their method of attack. Watch them while you jump rope or shadow box.
4. When sparring, try different moves and techniques and remember the reaction of your sparring partner. If he/she responds the same way more than twice, he/she probably has developed a habit that you can expose. Expose it by luring him/her into a position of vulnerability (by throwing the same punches as before, or by feinting those punches), and then counterpunching. This will also improve the quality of your sparring partners, especially if you inform them of what you did after the session is over. Making them better will in turn make you a better boxer.
5. When boxing, be patient. Throw feints to gauge the reaction of your opponent. Control the tempo and progression of the bout, and always pay careful attention to the reaction of your opponent. Remember, a good boxer may be trying to fool you. Don't depend completely on a read—you could be wrong, or they could be tricking you. Always keep your guard up and be prepared for any reaction from your opponents. Don't be predictable, since your opponent may also be trying to read you!

Maintain your focus in the ring.

The Importance of Safety

Boxing is statistically safer than sports like hockey, football, and swimming. However, boxing can be a dangerous sport if participants do not follow important rules and guidelines. Listed below are five guidelines you should follow in order to decrease your chance of injury.

Protect Your Head

Medical literature suggesting that boxing can cause harm focuses almost exclusively on damage to the head. Medical evidence suggests that prolonged trauma, such as frequent sparring, may cause damage to some people.

Since the head houses your brain, protecting your head should be important both to you and your coach. You protect your head in two ways: 1) by wearing headgear, and 2) by keeping hits to the head at a minimum (you do this by being a skilled boxer). Your coach protects your head in two ways: 1) teaching you how to protect yourself, and 2) being prepared to stop a bout in which you are taking an excessive number of punches to the head. You and your coach should agree that voluntarily stopping a bout may be necessary in some cases. It is a mistake to allow an attack to continue simply to save face, for instance, in a tough bout. Stop the bout if a mismatch is obvious. Think of a loss as an opportunity to work harder and win the next time.

Take defense seriously. Practice defense at least as much as you practice your offense. It may not be glamorous, but defense will win bouts and will reduce your likelihood of getting hurt. Practice moving your head to avoid being an easy target, slip punches, parry or catch punches, duck, and move your legs. If you move your head properly, you will get hit less often.

Don't spar every day. In lieu of sparring, many coaches prefer to keep a watchful eye on their boxers when they hit the heavy bag, work one-on-one with the focus mitts, and perform one-step-sparring drills with a teammate.

Once boxers are to the point they can spar, they only need to spar a few of the days they go to the gym if they are preparing for competition. Sparring can be a helpful exercise, but it is fruitless if boxers cannot work well, either because they are not in shape, or because they don't have the skills to protect themselves or score blows. Once you are to the point you can start to spar, don't forget to continue with the exercises that developed those skills in the first place. Boxers who only go to the gym to spar are "gym fighters," and they tend to be unsuccessful in actual bouts.

Protect Your Mouth

The teeth and jaw are protected by a mouthpiece and by your ability to do two things: protect your head and keep your mouth closed.

You must keep your mouth closed when you box. If you get hit when your mouth is open (even slightly) you increase the chance of damaging your teeth, and of dislocating or even breaking your jaw. You don't have to clench your teeth to get good closure on your jaw; just keep your teeth together. Many boxers fail to do this because they are out of shape, and become out of breath: then the natural reaction is to open your mouth in order to get more oxygen to your lungs. Develop cardiovascular fitness so that you don't have to gasp for breath while in the ring.

There are several styles and types of mouthguards from which to choose. Generally, the mouthpiece must be comfortable and fitted properly to perform well. Styles, type, thickness, fit, and maintenance of your mouthpiece are discussed below.

Style: There are two basic styles of mouthguards: top-only and top/bottom teeth guard. The top-only style is sufficient for boxing. The top/bottom style is designed with a hole through the middle of the sets of teeth so that you can breathe through your closed mouth. Often times this breathing hole is not large enough for a lot of boxers, and they open their mouths to gasp for air. Doing this makes the double mouthpiece virtually useless. The double-fit is also cumbersome—it's hard to communicate with coaches or officials when it is in place.

Type: There are two kinds of fitted mouthguards, and both work well: the store-bought mouthpiece (boiled to mold to your teeth) or a dentist-made mouthpiece (in which an impression of your teeth is used as a mold). Most serious boxers prefer the dentist-made mouthpiece because it is a better fit and is usually thinner than store-bought mouthguards. The downside to dentist-made mouthpieces is that they are expensive, therefore be sure to tell your dentist what you want and need. There are some companies that will send you a kit to make the impression of your teeth at home, for you to mail the kit back for the mouthpiece to be created.

Thickness: The mouthpiece actually serves to unify your teeth so that they are strengthened by each other: a blow is displaced through all of your teeth, rather than being focused on just one. Thickness is less important than a good fit.

Fit: A good fit will ensure that the mouthguard stays in place. If you should happen to get hit while your mouth is open, a good fit will prevent the mouthpiece from slipping into the back of your throat, or coming out of your mouth.

Maintenance of your mouthpiece: Keep your mouthpiece clean by rinsing it after each use, and by washing it regularly. Keep the piece in a container (plastic bags aren't very good because moisture cannot easily escape the bag). Don't let people handle your mouthguard (if you know you may need it, put it in at the beginning of your workout and leave it in). If your guard falls on the floor, wash it off. And finally, don't let anyone else use your mouthpiece.

Protect Your Body

There are several organs that are protected by having good defense and by wearing a groin protector. Although the groin protector was originally developed to protect the exposed genitalia of male boxers, it also may serve to protect the kidneys, some of the stomach, and the intestines. Thus, a protector that is a wrap-around design, may provide an advantage over those that serve only as a shield for the groin area. A well-fitted groin protector will reach as high as the navel (bellybutton) and snugly fit all the way around the body.

There is no medical evidence to suggest that trauma to the breast will result in any harm to breast tissue. No boxer, male or female, has yet been known to develop breast cancer as a result of boxing. Most professional boxing commissions make breast protectors mandatory because they assume that the breast needs special protection. Most governing bodies make groin protectors optional for women. Women boxers who wear groin protectors have an advantage in the ring, since their lower stomach is protected.

If a commission requires women to wear breast protectors, you may find flexible or foam cups that can be slipped into a sports bra the most comfortable and least obtrusive. Hard, plastic shield-like protectors are cumbersome, make you a bigger target, and tend to shift in the course of a bout. Hard plastic shields and cups have also been known to cut and chafe wearers.

Protect Your Hands

As important as the hands are in boxing, it is perplexing why some boxers would still hit heavy bags and spar without handwraps and gloves. Handwraps are 2 x 120-220-inch bands of cloth that are wrapped around the wrist, knuckles, and thumb of each hand. No boxer should participate in any boxing activity without the protection that well-placed handwraps can provide. Handwraps give you extra protection you may need for your wrist, knuckles, and thumbs. Handwraps do not ensure that you will not hurt your hands, but not using handwraps is a sure invitation to disaster.

In competition, gauze or Velpeau is used. Tape is used at a minimum and it is never placed over the knuckles. This rule prevents people from building "tape casts" that would encase the hand in a shell, and thus make it dangerous to an opponent. For examples of ways to wrap your hands for competition or workouts, go to the next essay, entitled "Techniques for Wrapping Hands."

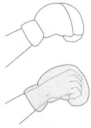

Proper position of hand in glove

The gloves you use should also be safe. When hitting bags and focus mitts, or when sparring, be sure to use gloves that are big enough to give you (and your workout partner) plenty of padding. The gloves should also fit snugly so that your hand does not slip around inside the glove. When putting on gloves, be sure your thumb and knuckles are set firmly inside the glove. Gloves with visible tears or cracks in the leather should not be used in sparring drills, since they may cause an abrasion or a cut to your opponent's skin or eyes.

Make Smart Decisions

Finally, as a boxer you have to make smart decisions about your health. You should not take part in any athletic activity (including boxing) until you have cleared it with your healthcare provider. Keep your coaches up to date on how you are feeling so that they can make adjustments to your training schedule. In any activity, and boxing is no exception, symptoms such as light-headedness or headaches should be checked out by a physician. Take pre-bout physicals seriously and let the ringside physician know if you are hurt or don't feel well.

Listen to your body. If your body hurts, it may be tired or strained. There is a difference between good pain and bad pain. Good pain is that uncomfortable feeling you get when you're on your last lap, your last lift, your last round, or when you are pushing yourself to go faster than before. This is the kind of pain that makes you stronger and faster. This pain is temporary. It is the kind of pain you should work through if you want to be a better boxer.

Bad pain is the result of strain or extreme fatigue. Bad pain happens when you think you really hurt something or felt something "pop" in your body. Bad pain is uncomfortable and worrisome. Bad pain is the result of damage—also known as injury—to your body. Injuries can often turn chronic if not taken seriously and treated.

Though a physician should make the final determination as to whether you have a serious injury, you must learn to listen to your own body and know when the pain you are experiencing is good or bad. All champions learn to love the good pain and also know when to take time out for recovery from injuries.

Weight:
Weight Loss and Making Weight

Boxing competitors are matched according to experience level and weight. Though weight categories may shift somewhat between matched bouts, tournaments, and international competition, boxing is based on weight class systems such as those in Tables 3.1, 3.2 and 3.3.

Notice there are no provisions for height or body type. This means that someone who weighs 165 pounds could presumably be from 5' to 6'0" tall. Generally, though, heights will increase as weight increases. For this reason boxers often try to lose as much weight as possible in order to have a height advantage in the ring. Another reason boxers try to drop to their lowest weight possible is because they believe they will be stronger than their opponents at a lighter weight. It is commonly believed the hardness of punches increases with weight (heavyweights hit harder than lightweights). Heavier boxers literally have more body mass to put behind their punches,

Different body types at the same weight

The Science of Boxing

Table 3.1
2002 Weight Classes for Amateur Boxing

Weight Classes	Upper Limit in lbs.	Upper limit in kilos.
Light Flyweight	106	48
Flyweight	112	51
Bantamweight	119	54
Featherweight	125	57
Lightweight	132	60
Light Welterweight	141	64
Welterweight	152	69
Middleweight	165	75
Light Heavyweight	178	81
Heavyweight	201	91
Super Heavyweight	201+	91+

Table 3.2
Previous Weight Classes for Amateur Boxing

Weight Classes	Upper Limit in lbs.	Upper limit in kilos.
Light Flyweight	106	48
Flyweight	112	51
Bantamweight	119	54
Featherweight	125	57
Lightweight	132	60
Light Welterweight	139	63.5
Welterweight	147	67
Light Middleweight	156	71
Middleweight	165	75
Light Heavyweight	178	81
Heavyweight	201	91
Super Heavyweight	201+	91+

Table 3.3
Typical Weight Classes for Professional Boxing

Weight Classes	Upper limit in lbs.
Strawweight	105
Jr. Flyweight	108
Flyweight	112
Jr. Bantamweight	115
Bantamweight	118
Jr. Featherweight	122
Featherweight	126
Jr. Lightweight	130
Lightweight	135
Jr. Welterweight	140
Welterweight	147
Jr. Middleweight	154
Middleweight	160
Super Middleweight	168
Light Heavyweight	175
Cruiserweight	190
Heavyweight	190+

have larger muscles, and have longer fulcrums from which to generate power. Due to these factors, boxers try to be as light as possible without compromising their own strength and/or speed.

Body types vary. Some people have more dense bones than others; some athletes hold more muscle mass than others, and some boxers hold more water. All of these elements have to be considered before you attempt to manipulate your weight. See a nutritionist, physician, or nurse if you want to change weight classes. Go over, with an expert, how you feel at certain weights. Though there are some general recommendations about eating habits and body mass, do not settle for generic guidelines (like a "norm" chart). Generic guidelines for weight/height averages do not necessarily mean a weight is correct for you. Ask the expert you speak with to also consider any unique qualities of your own body, such as your caloric intake, muscularity, workout schedule, etc. Be an educated consumer of the information they share with you.

The Importance of Water

Most boxers desire to drop weight classes, however losing weight can be a long road for most people. Losing weight requires monitoring food intake (both the amount and type of food) as well as exercising regularly. Estimate weight loss at a maximum rate of one to two pounds per week. Plan ahead if you need to make weight for a bout or tournament. It is unfortunate that some boxers try to lose weight quickly by dehydrating: wearing rubber or vinyl suits, not drinking water, and/or spitting excessively. They falsely assume that water, nutrients, and rest can be replenished after the weigh-in. Some boxers even brag that they can gain as much as eight pounds between the weigh-in and their bout. The fact is, water is necessary for chemical reactions in the body such as increases in metabolism. Denying your body water may create an imbalance detrimental to your health.

Dehydration of just one to two percent of your body weight (that's only 1.5 to 3 pounds for a 150-pound person) can negatively affect your athletic performance and lead to slowed reflexes, decreased strength, decreased oxygen use, decreased aerobic power, and decreased speed. Greater dehydration can lead to loss of coordination, impaired judgement, and sometimes even death. Wrestling is a sport that also uses weight classes. Some wrestlers have died as a result of trying to "cut weight" using dangerous methods of eliminating water from their bodies. You severely handicap your strength, speed, and recovery in the ring if you have dehydrated yourself to make weight.

The National Athletic Trainer's Association suggests athletes (and their coaches) watch for the following warning signs of dehydration: thirst, irritability, headache, weakness, dizziness, cramps, nausea, and decreased performance. Being dehydrated can cost you your bout, or if prolonged can lead to serious problems with your health, including susceptibility to heat stroke.

To decrease the possibility of heat stroke and dehydration, you should: 1) drink about 8 ounces of water prior to working out, 2) wear loose-fitting clothes when you work out, 3) schedule rest and water breaks every 15 minutes during workouts, 4) replace your wet clothes with dry ones during long workouts, and 5) drink enough water to replace what you have lost during your workout. If you lose one pound during a workout, drinking 16 ounces of water will replace the water you lost. Don't replace lost fluids with one giant "chug," since large amounts of water will empty through your system more quickly than small amounts.

Your body needs energy, water, and rest to operate effectively. If you deny your body these things, you are compromising your health and your ability to perform well in the ring. Drink water before, during, and after exercising.

Some Other Points About Food

There are many books that can give you a good idea about what foods make a well-balanced diet (or visit the USDA's web site at www.usda.gov). Your healthcare provider can give you pamphlets and advice about what is best for you. However, here are several simple food secrets that over the years have proved to be helpful for boxers.

Focus on foods you need. When trying to lose weight, focus on the foods you need to consume, rather than think about the foods you shouldn't eat. Changing your focus will help change your choices, and set you on a path to healthy eating.

Maintain adequate levels of potassium. Bananas are a good source of potassium, as are prunes, raisins, cantaloupe, avocado, and grapefruit. Potassium aids recovery time from injury and even helps prevent muscle cramps. Two helpings of potassium-rich foods per day are adequate.

Don't drink milk the day of your bout. Milk and other milk products such as cheese and ice cream can sometimes coat your mouth and throat with a film making it a little more difficult to swallow or clear your throat. Mucus production is also increased and thickened by milk and milk products, potentially making it more difficult to breathe. If you can live without it, don't drink milk the day of competition.

Drink water. Compared to water, sports drinks may taste good, but the carbohydrates they contain take longer to absorb into your system. They are also typically loaded with sugar and flavoring that can coat the mouth and throat. Pure water is the natural and economical way to satisfy your body's needs.

Eat pre-bout meals that you like. You can eat just about any of your favorite foods you choose the day of your bout. However, it is best (for your stomach's sake) that you stay away from particularly spicy, greasy, or fatty foods. Your last light meal should be consumed about two to five hours before you box so that you've had plenty of time to digest. Don't stuff yourself, but eat enough to eliminate hunger. Preferably, eat foods that also contribute to hydration, such as fruits. If you are travelling away from home for your bout, you may need to pack your food since you won't know what is available at the venue.

> **Take care of your body,
> and your body will take care of you.**

Techniques for Wrapping Hands

There are 27 bones in the hand and wrist, and 60 different muscles which give the hand its flexibility, dexterity, and strength. Bones, muscles, and ligaments allow the hand to open and make a fist, and keep the wrist from collapsing when striking a target. The hand is strongest in the closed position (as a fist); therefore, the use of handwraps should facilitate making a fist by providing support at the wrist and thumb, and padding at the knuckles.

Any soft material can be used as a handwrap. The three most common handwrap materials are cotton fabric, cotton gauze, and Velpeau. Cotton fabric and Velpeau are most economical, since they can be washed and reused repeatedly. Many cotton fabric (training) handwraps contain a strip of Velcro to secure the wrap. Also, some cotton fabric wraps are mixed with elastic to provide more compression.

Handwrapping is an artful skill. There are dozens of ways to wrap your hands for workouts and competition. The way you wrap your hands will depend on the length of material you are using, the thickness of the material, and where you prefer to focus padding and/or tension in the wrap for your knuckles, wrist, and thumb.

The three examples provided here can be used as basic guides to wrapping hands. Experiment with variations of these examples, and make up a wrap of your own based on the strategies you see here.

The first two diagrams can be used for traditional training handwraps in lengths that range from 170 to 220 inches. The third example is provided for Velpeau wraps using only 2.5 meters of material.

REMINDERS FOR WRAPPING HANDS:
- The three focus areas for wrapping hands are the knuckles, wrist, and thumb.
- Keep the material flat on your hand to prevent uncomfortable lumps.
- Keep the fabric taut so the handwrap does not come undone in the course of a workout or a bout.
- Make a fist several times throughout the course of wrapping your hands to make sure the wrap is not too tight.
- Don't wrap too high on the wrist—wrist support is provided most effectively at the base of the wrist.
- If needed, use athletic tape to secure handwraps around the wrist, or tuck the end of the wrap into your palm to prevent unraveling.

The Ultimate Boxer

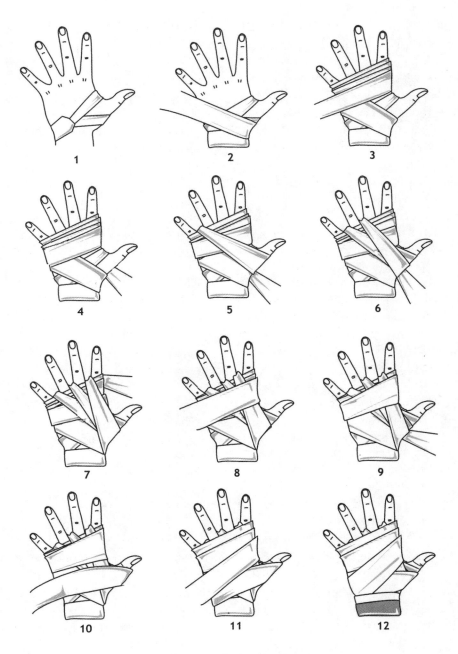

Simple wrap with cotton handwraps

The Science of Boxing

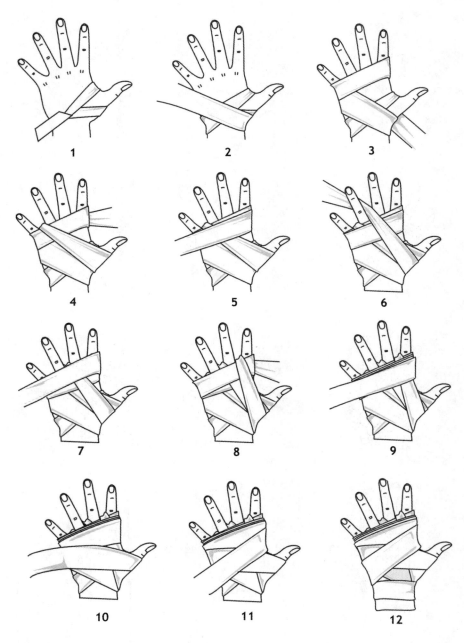

Advanced wrap with cotton handwraps

The Ultimate Boxer

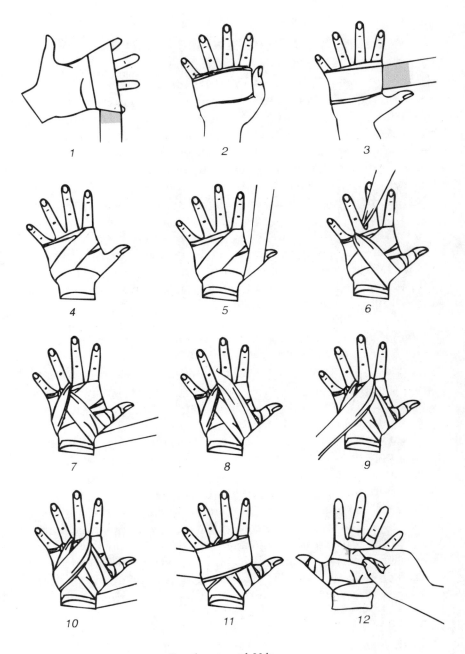

Sample wrap with Velpeau

Boxer's Code of Conduct: Fouls, Infractions, and the Referee's Duty

In boxing there are many rules and regulations designed to keep the sport safe and enjoyable for participants. Some boxers do not know the rules, and others disobey rules simply because they are tired, inexperienced, or sloppy boxers. Still others, worried that they may lose a bout, commit fouls in an effort to best their opponent. Because fouls are dangerous, it is the referee's duty to impose standards of fair play on the bout. The referee's vantage point allows him/her to see fouls you may commit. If you are warned for violating a rule, correct your problem immediately to avoid penalty by officials.

The referee will indicate when you have violated a rule either in a break or after stopping the action momentarily. If you are cautioned about violating a rule more than twice, you will be warned, and point(s) may be deducted. If the problem is still not corrected, you may be subject to disqualification.

Keep in mind that officiating is a subjective skill, and some referees are particularly sensitive to certain rule infractions. All referees have a certain officiating style: how much distance they keep from boxers, how they move, and the way they demonstrate the foul committed (amateur referees will not talk during the bout, they only demonstrate the fouls). Be confident that most referees try their best to make the bout fair and safe.

If you wish to indicate that a foul was unintentional, bow quickly to your opponent from a safe distance. Your opponent will be less likely to take the foul personally, and judges and referees will make mental note that you apologized for the offense.

There is one foul boxers often commit on purpose: the hold. Referees and judges get frustrated with boxers who hold frequently— it makes the job of officiating more difficult. Additionally, it is dangerous since you are unable to protect yourself when you are reaching for a hold. You can take advantage of opponents that hold by pushing them off with your shoulder, and countering quickly with a punch. For example, if your opponent is resting on your left shoulder, give him/her a quick push with the shoulder, then counter with the cross.

Finally, if you are in a bout in which your opponent is committing fouls but the referee is not calling the infractions, do not complain to the referee about the problem. Complaining to the referee generally highlights your own actions in the ring. For example, if your opponent is leading with the head, and you keep his/her head down with your elbow (to prove a point to the referee), then you can almost guarantee that you will be called for holding. Rather than complain about a dirty boxer, make sure he or she pays for infractions by capitalizing on the bad form. For example, if your opponent likes to hold, then give a feint forward, wait for his/her hands to come out to grab you, and strike him/her. If your opponent leads with his/her head, or lowers his/her head too much, strike the top of the head. Focus on winning the round. Learn the rules and the referee's signals for rule infractions. Obey the rules and boxing will be a much more enjoyable experience for you, your coach, and your fans.

Common Fouls and Referee Signals in Olympic-style Boxing

Boxing is a sport, not a fight. To box well you should be careful not to commit fouls. Fouls can be broken into five major categories: illegal use of the head, holding, illegal offensive maneuvers, illegal defensive maneuvers, and illegal actions on the part of the corner (coaches). When an amateur boxer commits a foul, he/she will be cautioned by the referee who will use a hand signal to identify the foul and caution the boxer not to commit the foul again. These hand signals will mimic the infraction. If a boxer continues to commit fouls, then the referee will warn him/her, and point(s) may be taken away from his/her overall score.

The illustrations below were created by USA Boxing, Inc., in order to help boxers and coaches understand the fouls and the signals that referees use to caution and warn boxers. These are some of the most common fouls in amateur boxing. For more information on amateur rules and regulations, visit the USA Boxing website at www.usaboxing.org or AIBA at www.aiba.net. For listings of fouls in professional boxing, consult the local boxing commission in your area.

The Science of Boxing

Ducking below the beltline

Leading with the head (head butting)

Holding with one arm

Holding below the belt

Holding with clenched arms

Pulling and hitting

Holding and hitting

Slapping

Hitting below the belt

Hitting the opponent's back

Hitting the back of the head

Illustrations on page 132 and 133 courtesy of USA Boxing, Inc.

The Ultimate Boxer

Hitting with the elbow

Hitting with the forearm

Pressing with forearm

Kneeing the opponent

Hitting a boxer who is down

Passive defense

Any use of the ropes

Pushing

Hanging onto opponent

Wrestling

Both boxers wrestling

Coaching from the corner or inciting someone to do so

Illustrations on page 132 and 133 courtesy of USA Boxing, Inc.

Chapter Four
Gaining the Strategic Advantage

The Rhythm of the Boxing Zone

Establishing your distance is probably the most difficult skill in boxing. Distance is the amount of space between you and your opponent in which you can effectively put him/her at the end of your punches. The end of your punch has the most "pop" because you are able to snap your punches. Smothering punches by being too close to your opponent will not result in effective scoring blows. Being too far away from your opponent means you will completely miss him/her, or expose yourself if you reach too much to make contact.

The boxing zone is that space in which you can hit and be hit, it is the space in which you and your opponent have your respective distance. In this zone, you are engaged with your opponent. Both of you are vulnerable. You have the ability to score and use defensive tactics in order to keep from being scored upon. Develop your ability to focus on your offense, defense, and strategy without being distracted. Integrate your offense and defense together to be effective in the boxing zone.

The safest place to be in the sport of boxing is out of the range of your opponent's attack; however, this also puts you out of scoring range. Therefore, the best strategy is to move in and out of the boxing zone quickly and effortlessly, strongly and efficiently, with confidence and with alertness. Accomplish this with the v-step, the in-and-out movement, the side step, and by staying in constant motion.

The boxing zone is the space in which both boxers are within striking distance of each other.

You should always aim for efficiency in movement: punches, feints, steps, and defensive maneuvers. The distance between you and your opponent changes constantly during the course of a match; strive to make your movements in and out of range flow seamlessly.

All matches have a certain rhythm. In a match between novice boxers, a rhythm may be difficult to distinguish, but for the very skilled, a boxing match may closely resemble a dance. Boxers move forward and backward, moving together, then apart. Boxers follow each other around the square ring, mirroring the other in almost perfect reverse. Boxers have grace that is tempered by the quick strike of gloves. Once you understand the rhythm of your own movement, in a round and in a match, you can begin to influence the rhythm of the match to your benefit. Changing the rhythm of a round or match can disrupt the focus of your opponent. Changing the direction of your movement, and the tempo or variety of punches, may serve to break one rhythm and begin a new one.

Another kind of rhythm is momentum. Momentum is a powerful force that can take over and blur the recent history of your match. Put momentum on your side: end every round by scoring and remaining strong in your movement and punches. Judges are impressed by this show of ability and your opponent will not forget a strong finish during the minute-long rest.

> **Waste no energy in the ring, and save none for the ride home.**

Maximizing Your Defense

A good defense is the basis for an effective offense; and your offense, when executed properly, will promote effective defense. Developing these complementary components requires practice. The following points will aid you in this endeavor.

Guard against the jab. Many ill-prepared boxers go into bouts thinking offense will win. It may work for your first few bouts, but this strategy will not work against boxers that counter your offense and absorb blows by guarding and blocking. If you miss the defense on a jab, you will be ill-prepared to handle the rest of the combination that follows. Prepare yourself to parry, catch, slip, duck, take a half-step back, or sidestep the jab. Practice all of these defensive moves against someone with a solid jab. Once you have learned to defend well, think about how you would counter a good jab. The most effective counters include a simultaneous jab (as you parry or duck, for example), or a well-timed and well-placed counter (such as a hook or a cross to the body).

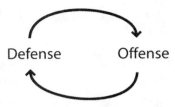

Defense leads into offense, and offense leads into defense.

Stay light on your feet so you can move anytime and in any direction without warning or preparation. Focus on finding good balance and keeping your legs bent. In a good boxing stance, you should be able to move to your right, left, back, or forward effortlessly and powerfully. Practice by moving your feet, not just your head and body to elude punches. Use defensive strategies that allow you to stay within range so you can score or create openings.

Keep your eyes open. It is a natural reflex to close your eyes (blink) when something—like a fist—comes flying at your face. As a boxer, you have to retrain your eyes to stay open when punches come at you. Keep your eyes open so you can see what is being thrown, in order to defend against it. If you are in the habit of blinking, your opponent will attempt to take advantage of your temporary blindness. Concentrate on your eyes the next time you do a one-step sparring exercise (like the throw-and-catch drill) with a partner.

Keep your chin tucked. Tucking your chin reduces the likelihood of sustaining serious injury: it keeps the throat unexposed; it makes the nose and chin less of a target; and it makes the forehead (protected by headgear) absorb any punches not defended adequately. Keeping the chin down also helps put the rest of your body in a position from which you can move and attack effectively.

Though the various kinds of defense have been discussed elsewhere in this book, the exercises below are designed to improve your efficiency in each of the defensive areas. Use these exercises to practice defense perfectly. Then add offense to your defensive moves to practice the flow of defense and offense together.

EXERCISES FOR DEFENSE:

1. *Cross-the-ring rope duck.* As demonstrated in Figure 2.1, move up and down the length of the rope, using the duck in a u-dip fashion. If you can feel the rope making contact with your head and shoulders, you know your movement is efficient.
2. *Slip/slide on maze ball:* Swing the maze ball, being especially careful

not to move too far over to the side or to stay over too long to either side. Bend the legs, then quickly return to your original position.
3. *Check your reaction to feints:* Work with a partner, asking them to throw feints and jabs against you. Stay under control, being careful not to react to phantom punches.
4. *Defense-only sparring:* Find partners who are equally or less skilled than you, and allow them to work their offense against your defensive moves. Evade their attack with side steps, ducks, slips, and also catch their punches. Keep your eyes open as you watch the punches.
5. *Combinations of defense:* With someone holding focus mitts, work on transitioning combinations out of defensive moves. Evade a jab, cross, or hook, then throw a two-, three-, or four-punch combination. Change up your combinations, always maintaining the focus on defense and offense becoming synchronized.

The most dangerous punch is the one you don't see coming.

Defensive and Evasive Tactics

There are three other defensive tactics that help round out a defensive arsenal and keep you out of dangerous situations in the ring: clinching, getting off of the ropes, and moving out of corners.

Clinching. The clinch is a dangerous but common way to avoid being hit. The clinch occurs when boxers are infighting and their arms become tangled. Basically, one boxer will purposefully tie up the other's arms by holding (with straight arms) or lifting the arms under the opponent. Clinching is a foul. If both boxers are clinched, then the referee may only command "break." However, if it is clear one boxer is causing the clinch, the referee may caution or warn that boxer for holding. Clinching is dangerous since you can easily get hit when you are busy trying to reach for your opponent's arms or gloves. The best defense for a clinch or hold is to move in a jerking style, quickly down and backward from the opponent, then throw quick counters.

Getting off the ropes. When considering the ropes, the basic rule is to stay away from them. Boxing with your back against the ropes is dangerous because you limit your options for movement by at least 50 percent. Getting off the ropes takes a lot of energy because you must time your sideways movements. If your opponent throws a left hand, move to your right, since they will often be throwing a right-hand next. This will give you a small enough opening to sidestep while covered or punching. Sidestepping with a duck is even better since you may evade an oncoming punch. Another way to escape the ropes is to feint in one direction so your opponent will try to cut off your path, then move in the opposite direction. Counter immediately with an attack of your own to spin your opponent onto the ropes.

Never use the ropes to spring back into the center of the ring. Some boxers believe bouncing off the ropes will put an extra amount of power on their punch, but some boxers actually spring into their opponent's attack.

Moving out of the corners. The one thing worse than backing yourself into the ropes is backing yourself into a corner. In the corner you reduce your options for movement by at least 75 percent. If you do happen to find yourself in a corner, time your movement so you step to the side of the punch that was thrown. If your opponent throws a right hand, immediately step to your left at an angle next to your

Available movement off of the ropes.

opponent. Again, rotate toward your opponent and infight if you want to bully him/her into the corner you just escaped.

Another way to time your movement out of the corner is to briefly disrupt your opponent's attack with quick punches of your own. Your quick punches may disrupt your opponent's momentum and give you enough time to rapidly move around your opponent.

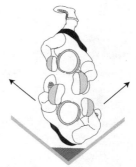

Available movement out of the corners.

Additional Evasive Tactics

Evasive tactics (moves in which you attempt to avoid being hit) include the side step, duck, and slip/slide. Two other evasive tactics that can be used for good effect are the weave and the roll.

Weaving. Weaving is the act of moving around punches so that you "weave" your body around them. You can weave yourself to the right and left, as well as forward and backward. The weave is a combination of a duck, a slip/slide, and a u-dip. Practicing the weave takes a keen eye and a lot of patience. Bobbing, similar to weaving, is the practice of ducking down and up to evade punches.

Rolling. Rolling is a movement (from the knees up) in which your body moves in the same direction as the punch. This either prevents you from being hit, or removes a great deal of the impact.

Use your knees, waist, and shoulders to "give" with the punch. Taking a step back or to the side may aid your roll (like a half-step back) and promote your offense, or put you in a better defensive position. With all of these defensive tactics, be sure to stay within boxing range so you can advance your own offense attack.

Rolling with the punch: moving in the same direction as the punch so as to evade or take the power off the punch.

Tough defense can force your opponent into leaving openings.

Angles, Angles, Angles

Most novice boxers only move forward and backward in a straight line; that's why many novice boxers get hit a lot in their bouts. Moving in any direction (except straight forward) in an approach to strike or evade the other boxer forms an angle. Used correctly, an angle is something that will give you the clear advantage in the ring. Offensive angles (used on the approach, and when engaged in boxing) and defensive angles (used as an evasive tactic, and to create openings) are discussed below.

Angles on Offense

The "angle on approach" occurs when you engage your opponent from an angle (a v-step) rather than meeting him/her directly. The concept of the v-step approach is to connect with your opponent, and then move out of range before he/she can hit you. The v-step is an in-and-out movement that resembles the letter V from a bird's-eye view.

With the v-step approach, avoid moving into punches. Be especially careful when approaching your opponent's strong side. Do not create a predictable pattern every time you move (always moving to the right and then the left, for instance). The constant movement of the v-step on approach is also known as the in-and-out style.

Another offensive angle can be created once you are engaged in the boxing zone. The step-in-and-over move situates you at your opponent's side and is usually best accomplished with a duck or a slip or slide. This step-over follows a punch, or a feint, or can also be used with a punch. For example, jab and step to the right at the same time. Your opponent does not expect you to move this way, and you will quickly move out of his/her range to get hit. From this angle, you can attack with body or head shots while your opponent tries to square back up to you.

Side step your opponent when you have him/her on the ropes or in the corner. Take angles when your opponent is trying to hold, or when you throw your jab. If you use angles in your attack, you can effectively "pick apart" your opponent and frustrate him/her into making more and more mistakes.

Another angled approach is the feint and side

V-step on approach

step. Rather than moving straight ahead, feint the step-in and instead move to the side (usually to the right of a right-handed opponent). Most boxers will fall for the feint by either moving backward (in which case you may follow and strike) or with a punch (in which case you are out of range of getting hit, and can counter the failed attack, especially if he/she overextends his/her punch).

Taking an angle to the right or left while engaged with opponent.

After taking an angle in the boxing zone, continue to circle around your opponent with a pivot of the front foot. This will force your opponent to find you in order to square up to you.

When using angles, you are literally attacking and moving on your opponent from different angles in order to find openings and discover a better boxing position. As your opponent moves around the ring, you will increase your options for angles that maximize offensive and defensive strikes. Constantly give your opponent something different to look at; always keep your opponent thinking about your location.

Angles on Defense

Defensive angles increase the effectiveness of defensive maneuvers, such as the slip/slide, duck, side step, parry, etc. Taking angles on defense keeps your opponent looking for you. If your opponent has to look for you, then he/she is neither comfortable nor properly protected. This makes your opponent vulnerable to your attack, as well: imagine looking for an opponent who has "disappeared" then surfaces as you turn to find him/her. Meet your opponent's turned head with a jab or power shot, and meet the exposed body with any punch that can land quickly. Working angles on defense creates openings for an offensive attack. Another angled defensive move is stepping over to either side of an advancing opponent. Aggressive boxers will move straight past you. A quick step-over, followed by a pivot turn as your opponent moves straight forward, will produce an angle from which you can quickly attack at minimal risk to yourself. Defense and offense are most effective when you take angles to increase your movement opportunities in the ring. The one-step

Taking an angle for defensive purposes can turn into an offensive attack.

sparring drills listed below are designed to develop your skills in taking angles.

ONE-STEP SPARRING DRILLS TO PRACTICE ANGLES:

1. Alternate throwing two jabs and catching two jabs, while you circle (pivot) only to your partner's weak side. The best defense in this drill is catching/parrying the two jabs, or you can slip or duck the second jab. Vary the tempo of your jabs to keep your opponent alert.
2. Throw two jabs to the head, but take an angle to your right while you throw the second jab. The jab should make contact before the front foot hits the ground. Advance quickly and in position to throw to the body, or pivot and throw a combination. The defense for this sequence could include a catch for the first jab and a side step (to the right) to get out of the way of the second blow.
3. In the open ring, practice the v-step approach. Keep your hands up. Do not always keep the rhythm of the "v" consistent because this pattern will be easy for your opponent to read. For good defense be sure to keep hands up, move the head, and sidestep. Watch your opponent for a pattern, then time the rhythm in order to punch or evade any punch in his/her arsenal.
4. With your sparring partner on the ropes or in the corner, practice throwing a variety of body and head shots while continuously alternating to each side of your opponent. Keep your feet moving and use u-dips and half-steps to vary your angles. For defense, use the cover, and time a side step if there is an opening.

> **You can't be hit if you can't be seen.**

Variations on the Fundamentals

There are many ways to capitalize on sound fundamentals. Below are several techniques that build on your knowledge of the jab, defense, feints, bout control, tempo change, reads of opponents, and several other elements that can give you an advantage in the ring.

The jab is the most often-thrown punch. It helps establish distance, it initiates most combinations, and it can be thrown at a safe distance without exposing the rest of your body. Take advantage of the way your opponents throw their jab. For example, if your opponent doesn't bring his/her jab back in a straight line, beat their jab back to their face with a jab of your own, or even with a quick overhand cross. Anyone can use this technique if they time it precisely, but it takes practice to develop the correct timing.

Another way to take advantage of a poor jab is to manipulate it. A lazy jab is one that is thrown without authority and returns in a lackadaisical style. Use your catch to control the jab as it meets your glove. With your wrist and hand, turn the jab down or to the inside. If you turn the jab down, you can throw to your opponent's head with a jab or even your power hand. Perform the catch and cross using a continuous motion so your punch actually begins with the push of your opponent's glove. When pushing to the inside, you can move your opponent's entire arm across his/her body. This action will freeze up his/her other attack and will give you an opportunity to throw a jab or cross to the head, or even combine it with a side step to throw a long hook or a cross to the body. Do not attempt to control someone's jab until you have mastered the catch/parry, or you risk completely missing the catch.

Use your jab. Bouts can be won with an effective jab, especially with change-up jabs. Use the traditional jab, as well as the upper jab and the blinding jab, to keep your opponent off guard. The upper jab (also known as the splitter) is thrown exactly the same way as a traditional jab, but at 95 percent extension of the arm the hand is turned in the opposite direction so the palm is facing upward. The upper jab may catch your opponent off guard, since your jab will be traveling upward and will likely penetrate the defense of your opponent. The upper jab can be used as a lead jab, or within a combination.

The jab can also be used to temporarily "blind" your opponent to your next offensive or defensive move. Blinding jabs are successive jabs thrown at the head that return only halfway to the starting position.

Gaining the Strategic Advantage

This technique may frustrate your opponent because he/she will be temporarily blinded by your extended glove. Holding the arm outstretched toward your opponent without bringing the punch halfway back to the starting position may be grounds for a posting foul.

Boxer with jab extended

Another variation on the jab is the stiff jab. The stiff jab puts directed power on the end of the punch as you advance toward your opponent. A stiff jab is useful when attempting to back a weaker opponent into a corner or onto the ropes. The stiff jab requires the hand to stay extended for a longer period of time, so be careful when using this strategy, since it makes you more vulnerable to a counter or a parry.

Boxer with upper jab extended

The feint is extremely effective, especially against novice boxers. For the advanced boxer, though, feints may be more commonplace in a bout. As an advanced boxer, you can use the feint against a feinter. Feint the punch or move your opponents expect from you (if you were to fall for their feint), and they will counter your feint and leave themselves open for attack. If you can think three or more steps ahead—imagining what counters, and counter for counters, could be thrown—feinting at feints puts you in a position to control the bout.

Stay in control of the bout. Control the rhythm of the match by focusing on and by changing the number, timing, tempo, power, and speed of your punches. Force your opponent to move in different directions. Keep changing your punches and the combinations in which they are thrown. Change your defense sometimes, too, by reacting in different ways to jabs and power punches.

Don't box predictably. Make use of all the skills you know every time you box. The practice will make you more comfortable with various techniques and the change of pace and style will keep your opponent off guard. A good boxer utilizes quick changes, a variety of punches and defense, and has speed in footwork and punches.

Keep your opponent guessing about your attack by varying your targets. Throw punches upstairs (to the head) as well as downstairs (to the body). Be sure to also throw punches both to the inside (up the middle) and outside (around the sides) of your opponent, within a combination or series of combinations. If you vary your attack, your opponent will never have a chance to rest.

The Ultimate Boxer

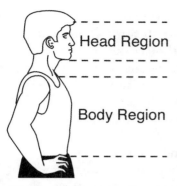

Upstairs and downstairs target zones of opponents

Another strategy is switching between the right and left-handed boxing stances. Switching immediately after a combination which ends in a side step can confuse an opponent. By the time your opposition squares back up to you, you will be in a different stance, which your opponent may not recognize at first and thus not be prepared to box or defend against you adequately.

When necessary, force openings. You will, from time to time, have to make openings happen, particularly when boxing opponents who cover well. One way is to feint. However, not all boxers will fall for the feint. Another way to make openings is to hit the gloves or elbows of your opponent at an angle (from the inside to the outside) so as to, for a split second, create a small opening in which to throw a straight punch. Your timing and precision are key to sneaking something past your opponent's guard. Practice this technique of forcing openings with another skilled boxer, so that you get the feel for your opponent's reactions, as well as to estimate how much power you'll have to expand to open the elbows/gloves of potential opponents.

Watch your opponent for signs of fatigue or frustration. Good boxers learn to gauge the status of their opponent: they can tell when their opponent is tired, frustrated, or has been affected by a punch. If you can accurately read your opponent's, then you can act accordingly. There are reflexes in the body that telegraph our physical status. If a boxer is panting (out of breath), then attack before they can catch their breath. Watering and red eyes are a physiological response to being stung by a punch. Attack with scoring blows to overwhelm a threatened boxer. An alert referee will give a standing-eight count immediately. Frustrated boxers often furrow their brow, huff, or make comments in the ring. A frustrated boxer is likely to fall for feints, and this will make him/her even more

Inside and outside target zones of opponents

frustrated. Frustrated or angry boxers do not box well because they are overcome by emotion: they are no longer in control. Signs of fatigue in boxers include carrying the mouthpiece out of the mouth while breathing hard, and/or leaning on you while infighting or clinching. The best offense against a tired boxer is to press the action. Don't let your opponent rest if he/she is trying to take a break. Keep him/her moving by advancing with the jab, and keep punching when he/she is in close.

Keep your punches fast and sharp by paring them down. Make your punches economical—straight and quick. Eliminating extra moves in your punches, such as dropping the hand before you throw it, will also make your opponent less able to read you.

Punching with Power

Both hands must be able to punch with force. Directing your power in a controlled manner is a valuable offensive weapon. Though powerful punches will not count for extra points in amateur boxing, being able to punch with power may keep your opponent at bay and will allow you to change the tempo of combinations.

There are eight basic elements to throwing any punch with power:
1. Rapidly whip the hip, rotating the shoulder to extend the punch.
2. Shift your weight slightly to line up the body behind the punch.
3. Focus on punching with directed speed.
4. Aim one or two inches beyond the target.
5. Put the target on the end of your punch.
6. Throw straight punches, don't loop them.
7. Keep a short stance to generate sufficient tort in the hip.
8. Keep the muscles relaxed.

The best place to practice throwing powerful punches is on the heavy bag. Practice sound technique to avoid developing bad habits that may leave you vulnerable and compromise your ability to score points. Keep the following in mind:
- Don't telegraph the punch.
- Don't drop the fist off the cheek before you throw.
- Don't lose the speed of the punch by tensing your muscles.
- Don't overcommit to the punch by expecting to make contact.

Counterpunching, and Counters for Counters

The counter is simultaneously a defensive and an offensive tactic. A counter uses your opponent's attack to your benefit by taking advantage of the openings and weaknesses that are created by the attack. To counter well is an art and, to be effective, must be perfect in technique and in planning. Your timing, speed, and proper execution of the punch must all be in sync.

Bruce Lee, whose martial arts were influenced by boxing, said it best when he remarked: "For every lead, there is an opening, and for every opening, a counter, and for every counter, a parry or a counter-time." (*The Tao of Jeet Kune Do*, 72)

Indeed, there is always a counter, because there is always an opening made when a boxer attempts to punch another his/her opponent. Boxers are most vulnerable when they are punching, and you can learn to use this vulnerability to your advantage. The goal is to minimize your own openings while taking advantage of the openings of your opponents. For best results, use a counter when you see your opponent's punch, or as soon as you feel the pressure of your opponent's glove on you. If your opponent has made contact with you, then he/she is not in an effective defensive position. Take advantage of any vulnerabilities, such as a lazy defense, by countering quickly.

The counters below cover the straight jab, straight cross, the hook, and the uppercuts. This list is not exhaustive. It is simply meant to provide you with a starting point by which to experiment with counters and develop your own counterpunches for openings you see in sparring partners and in opponents.

Prepare for your opponent to counter your counters, whether in sparring or in competition. A boxer reacts to various actions in split seconds, so you should study punches, openings, and counters outside the ring, first. Visualize your counters. Practice your counters in front of a mirror, during shadowboxing, and in two-step sparring drills. Practicing perfectly will result in perfect execution of your skills. Your counters will then seem to come naturally in the course of a bout.

Additionally, the counters listed below should be practiced if the punch is thrown as a lead, at the end of a combination, or in the middle of a combination. Eventually you should become proficient enough to counter in the midst of your opponent's attack. To counter you must be on balance, therefore practice being comfortable in the boxing zone.

COUNTERS FOR A STRAIGHT JAB
- Stop their action with a jab of your own, aimed at the oncoming punch.
- Stop their action with a feint, either the jab or power hand; and throw a jab or cross after your opponent's reaction.
- Block or catch with the strong glove, step to your strong side and drive a straight jab to the chin or body.
- Block or parry to the outside and hook to the body or chin.
- Block or parry to the outside, duck and throw an uppercut to the chin.
- Parry to the inside guard position and uppercut to the solar plexus.
- Parry to the inside, then cross to the chin.
- Slip to outside, then throw a jab to the head or body.
- Slip to inside, duck, and throw a straight cross to the body or chin.
- Sidestep to the outside guard position and drive a cross to the chest, chin, or solar plexus.
- Duck and throw a jab or cross to the stomach.
- Take a half-step back and come back with a cross.

COUNTERS FOR A STRAIGHT JAB TO THE BODY
- Step at an angle away from the jab, but toward the opponent.
- Take a half-step back, and throw a hook to the head.
- Parry with the elbow, then throw either a jab or cross to the head.

COUNTERS FOR A STRAIGHT CROSS LEAD
- Catch, then throw a quick cross to the head.
- Parry to the inside, then drive a straight cross to the chin or body.
- Slip to the outside and shoot a cross to the chin or body.
- Sidestep to the outside and drive a cross to the chin or body.
- Roll with the punch, then come back with your own cross.
- Slip to the outside and land a hook to the solar plexus or chin.
- Sidestep to the outside and drive a hook to the chin or solar plexus.
- Sidestep to the outside and drive an uppercut to the chin.
- Shoulder block with a half-step back, then come back with your own cross to the head.

COUNTERS FOR A CROSS TO THE BODY
- Parry with the elbow and throw a hook to the head.
- Parry with the elbow and throw a straight cross to the head.
- Take a half-step back, then throw a cross to the head.
- Take half-step back, then uppercut to the head with your lead hand.

COUNTERS FOR A HOOK
- Throw a quick straight punch (#1 or #2) if the hook is wide.
- Throw a hook at the same time, if opponent drops their defensive hand.
- Duck under the hook and throw a #1, #2, or uppercuts to the body.
- Beat the hook by ducking and throwing an uppercut to the chin.
- Duck with half-step back and wait for hook to pass, then throw a straight counter punch.
- Block, then throw a cross to the head.

COUNTERS FOR A HOOK TO THE BODY
- Catch with the outside elbow, move into the punch, and throw a straight jab or cross to the chin.
- Take a half-step back, then straight punch to the head.

COUNTERS FOR AN UPPERCUT
- Catch with one hand and throw the opposite hand to the side of the chin that is exposed.
- Throw a body punch to the spot that the elbow just vacated when your opponent threw an uppercut.
- Throw a quick hook to the head at the same time.
- Take a half-step back, then move forward with a quick punch.
- Throw a straight punch to the chin if the opponent telegraphs the uppercut by dropping it off his/her chin.

The best way to minimize your own vulnerabilities when throwing counterpunches is to move in conjunction with your attack. Step to the side while punching. Move your head and body during, and especially after, a combination. Always be ready for a counter to your counter. Don't forget to relax when you counterpunch. When you stay relaxed you are more likely to make wise choices and to be accurate with your punches.

Counterpunching drills are important for building concentration in the ring. The best way to practice counterpunching is to work with a partner in two-step sparring drills. You can practice counterpunching drills with anyone as long as you both remember to throw your punches with speed, not power.

> **Good boxers practice like they want to perform.**

Punching to the Body

The body is a larger and more stationary target than the head. Many punches can be avoided simply by moving the head, but body punches are tougher to defend. To capitalize on your opponent's vulnerabilities, and to maximize your offensive attack, work combinations that involve punches to both the head and body. If you try to "head hunt" in the ring by only aiming for your opponent's head, you severely limit your offensive arsenal.

SIX REASONS TO PUNCH TO THE BODY:
1. You can score a point if the punch lands cleanly.
2. If a body punch is part of a combination, your chances of a judge seeing one scoring blow are increased.
3. If a body punch is part of a combination, different judges using computer scoring may see different scoring blows, but still within one second of each other.
4. Punching to the body may create openings to the head.
5. Body punches may tire your opponent.
6. Body punches worry your opponent and make him/her concentrate on defense, rather than offense.

Putting Your Skills to the Test: Sparring

The best way to test your competition skills is to spar. Sparring should be practiced under careful supervision, and minimally. Sparring too often is dangerous for three reasons: 1) trauma to the head should be minimized since repeated trauma may lead to injury, 2) your psychological health may be compromised if you continually put yourself in situations where you are frustrated with your sparring performance, and 3) sparring on a regular basis sometimes reinforces bad habits among boxers who become "too comfortable" in gym sparring sessions. Sparring should always be taken seriously and be recognized as a potentially dangerous activity. In order to experience the skill-building benefits of partnered sparring, without the dangers of all-out sparring, modular sparring exercises can be used. The purpose of putting limits on sparring is to 1) keep both boxers safe, and 2) practice specific skills so you master the skill of protecting yourself before moving on to free-form sparring and/or competition.

Preparing to Spar: One-step, Two-step, Directed Sparring

There are many functions of one-step, two-step, and directed sparring that help you become more comfortable with engaging in the act of boxing. Within the safe confines of a one-step drill you will learn how to keep your eyes open while boxing; become less afraid of your opponent's punches; learn how to move in the ring; get accustomed to your headgear, mouthpiece, and other safety gear; be able to gauge your fitness level; and become familiar and comfortable with specific skills.

In *one-step sparring*, both boxers take turns throwing and defending against one set of punches. Each boxer has strict instructions on what punches to throw and what defense to use in the ring. This exercise takes place in "real time"—boxers still throw quickly—however, their punches are severely limited. Each boxer knows precisely what punch the other will throw, but does not know the speed, power, or timing of the punches. Boxers alternate between offense and defense to help reinforce the transition of going immediately from offense to defense (and vice versa) in competition. One-step sparring can be done anywhere, but practicing in the ring can help you become accustomed to moving comfortably within its confines.

EXAMPLES OF ONE-STEP SPARRING EXERCISES:
1. Catch and parry jabs: alternate throwing two jabs as your partner parries your jabs, then your partner will throw two jabs as you work your defense. Pivot to the right or the left after you throw your punches.
2. Slip/duck jabs: alternate throwing two jabs as your partner slips or ducks your jabs, then your partner will throw two jabs as you slip or duck. Pivot to the right or the left after you punch.
3. Left and right catches: throw a jab and then a short cross as you partner parries the jab and then catches the cross. Duck or sidestep after you throw your punches.
4. Catch and duck the jab and hook: throw a jab and then a hook to the head while your partner catches the jab and ducks under the hook. Duck or pivot to the right/left after you throw your punches.
5. Catch and half-step back the jab and uppercut: throw a jab and then an uppercut with either hand to the head. Let your partner catch the jab and then take a half-step back to avoid the uppercut. Move at an angle to either side of your opponent after you throw your punches.
6. Catch and sidestep the double jab: practice taking angles by throwing two jabs while your opponent catches the first jab and side-

steps the second jab. Look for the opening on your partner's body and head when you step next to him/her. Pivot around your opponent after you throw your punches.
7. Catch the double jab and cross: throw a jab to the head, a jab to the body, and a cross to the head while your partner practices catching or slipping the first jab, catching the second jab with the elbow, and slip/half-step back/block the cross. Move around after you throw your punches.
8. Catch the jab and uppercut: throw two jabs to the head and an uppercut to the head while your opponent catches the jabs and catches the uppercut. Duck and move to either side after throwing punches.

Two-step sparring literally involves two steps of combinations in a drill. In one-step sparring you were focused on one combination and moving directly into defending against that same combination. In two-step sparring you will transition offense and defense into each other, as your opponent does the same. For example, you might throw two jabs and duck, while your opponent catches two jabs and throws a long hook to the head. In two-step sparring you punch or move while your opponent punches, and you work on quickly turning offense into an effective defense. Take an angle or pivot after you have finished a combination.

Practice two-step sparring drills slowly at first so that you and your partner know your specific offensive and defensive moves. Gradually you can build speed until you and your sparring partner are moving and punching at top speed.

Move around the ring between two-step sparring drills. As you re-set the drill, take a moment to slip, slide, duck, side-step, pivot, or even backpedal to re-set the drill in another part of the ring. Practicing movement in training will help you remember to move during a match.

The following six examples of two-step sparring are broken into components. Practice and perfect component A of a drill, then add component B, continuing to add components C through F until you have learned the complete exercise. For example, in the first exercise of Table 4.1, the red boxer will throw a jab, catch a jab, duck under a cross, throw a cross, elbow-block an uppercut to the body, and throw an uppercut to the body. Drills can also be altered to develop counterpunching skills and to defend against specific punches or moves. Of course, you can also make up your own counterpunching drills.

Table 4.1
Counterpunch Exercises for Two-step Sparring

		A		B	C	D	E	F
1	Red	1	catch	duck	2	elbow block	5 b	
	Blue	catch	1	2	slide	5 b	elbow block	
2	Red	1	1	elbow block	block	short 2	half-step back	
	Blue	parry	slip	2 b	3	block	short 2	
3	Red	1	1	slide	3	duck	block	
	Blue	parry	elbow block	2	catch	1	1	
4	Red	1	2	block	block	short 2	3 b	
	Blue	slip	slide	3	2	duck	elbow block	
5	Red	1	3	half-step back	2	elbow block	elbow block	
	Blue	catch	duck	1	slide	3 b	4 b	
6	Red	slip	elbow block	short 2	elbow block	block	short 2	sidestep left
	Blue	1	4	slide	3	3	duck	overhand 2

Directed sparring involves the handicapping of one or both boxers in order to maintain a safe and manageable sparring exercise. Both boxers can still move at top speed, but they work as a team as each focuses on specific skills (punches and/or defense). In directed sparring each boxer is given a set of instructions. Based on the instructions, each chooses when to throw punches, when to use different types of defense, and how fast or with what tempo to throw punches. This is the last step before advancing to free-form sparring.

EXAMPLES OF DIRECTED SPARRING EXERCISES:

1. Sparring using only the jab
2. Sparring with only the lead hand
3. Sparring with two-punch combinations, only
4. Sparring using only the v-step approach
5. Sparring while one person works on defense only
6. Sparring while one person punches only to the body
7. Shadow sparring using all punches (without touching the other boxer)

Free-Form Sparring

The final stage to sparring is the free-form sparring session which involves throwing punches, combinations, and using any defense necessary to score blows against your sparring partner. In free-form (or open) sparring, both boxers should remain controlled. If you are much better than your opponent, try to work on skills that are difficult for you, such as moving to your power side, slipping/sliding, taking angles, constant head movement, throwing uppercuts, or any other specific technique.

How Many Rounds?

While one-step and two-step sparring are exercises that can be used regularly at the gym, directed and free-form sparring should be practiced less frequently. It is generally believed you should free-form spar one or two more rounds than the number of rounds at which you compete: if you compete at three rounds, you could free-form spar four or five rounds in the gym to build physical and mental ring endurance. However, it is best to go for quality sparring, rather than quantity. If you can only box two rounds at a time before your technique diminishes significantly, then don't spar more than two rounds until you get into better shape. It is good to push yourself in sparring exercises, but remember that you will perform just like you practice. So, if you cannot spar with correct form, then limit the number of rounds you spar until you are in good enough condition to stay strong throughout the exercise. Round-robin sparring, sparring one or two rounds at a time, with a one-round break before you spar another one or two rounds, is a good strategy for getting work in the ring without compromising quality. Eventually you must get to the point you can spar a consecutive number of rounds equal or slightly greater than the number of rounds you will face in competition. Amateur boxers must remain active, explosive, and intense for the entire bout, and thus should practice like they expect to perform.

Additionally, if you box two-minute rounds, then you should spar two, two-and-a-half, or three-minute rounds. Sparring rounds that last much longer than your performance time will make you lazy in a match because you will have practiced at a slower pace. Box shorter rounds while you build your endurance. For example, start with three rounds of 90 seconds, and work up to four rounds of two-and-a-half minutes. To challenge your cardiovascular fitness, shorten your rest interval from one minute to 45 seconds.

Women and Men Sparring Together

Women and men may work together in sparring exercises. However, many women boxers (both professionals and amateurs) complain that boys and men sometimes try to "win" coed sparring sessions. If both boxers understand and follow the philosophy of sparring, coed practices should not be a problem.

Working Tough for Your Sparring Partner

Sparring partners should always be matched based on skill level, weight, and height. If there are no other options, mismatched boxers may have to work with each other. Take special care to one-step spar with new sparring partners before you step into the ring for a free-form sparring session, so that you have some notion of what to expect.

Finally, you are wasting your time and your sparring partner's time if you do not give your all in sparring and modular sparring drills. Stay focused and work on the skills that you and/or your partner set up at the beginning of the exercise. If you are tired enough to complain to your sparring partner, then wait to spar until you are recovered fully and can give your all to the exercise. Your sparring partner will only get better if you challenge him/her, and likewise, you depend on your sparring partner to challenge your skills and fitness.

In sparring, quality is much more important than quantity.

Working with a Novice Boxer in Sparring

Working with someone when sparring means that you collaborate to make the session productive for both of you. This implies you will not hurt your sparring partner, but rather will challenge him/her to improve. To accomplish this pull the power off your punches without compromising your form. Work both the body and head without knocking your partner down or out. Capitalize on mistakes your partner makes without making him or her feel stupid.

What is your sparring philosophy? What is your philosophy when boxing a novice? Think about your own expectations about sparring before you ask someone to actually step in the ring with you. If you want to spar in order to prove to someone that you are better, then challenge him/her to a real bout; don't try to prove it when sparring.

The guidelines below may help you communicate more effectively with a novice sparring partner. Better communication will result in better performance, and both of you will get improved results.

Basic Rules for Sparring with a Novice

- Spar with a novice after you have completed the rest of your day's workout. Begin the session a little tired so you can learn to stay focused even when you are tired and the edge is off your punches.
- Invite someone to spar with you. If you are a good boxer, novice boxers may hesitate to approach you. Invite a novice to work with you so he/she will feel welcome to ask for your help.
- Explain before the bell what you want to accomplish in the sparring session. Tell your partner how many rounds you want to work. Give specific instructions, based on your goals for the drill.
- Stay quick. Try to emulate the quickness that your partner will face in real competition.
- Pull the power off your punches so if they connect, they will not hurt your partner.
- Push your partner to throw many punches—stay in the boxing zone so that he/she will feel compelled to throw a lot. This is a great way to work on your defense.
- Work on your defensive moves such as the duck, slip, side step, and half-step back so that you get a good workout. Don't always evade punches by just moving out of range.
- Capitalize on your partner's mistakes to teach him/her the

consequences of bad technique. For example, catch and jab back quickly if your partner throws a lazy jab; or throw a short cross over an opponent with low hands.
- Don't always stop the action to explain what happened—doing so will interrupt the flow of the round and your partner will never get the benefit of working a complete round.
- Don't embarrass your partner by taunting him/her.
- Don't jump on your partner at the bell and intimidate him/her. Sometimes you should allow him/her to back you into a corner so that he/she can feel what it is like to be the aggressor, and you can improve your technique of getting out of corners.
- Move around a lot. Take angles in offense and defense. Make your partner work on footwork as much as on throwing punches.
- Don't commit fouls. Don't get lazy and hang onto your partner. Don't use the ropes. Don't hold and spin. Make the practice session similar to a competition, since novice boxers will likely emulate you in their bouts.
- Don't get too fancy or show off. Practice sound technique.
- Stay in good defensive position. Even the worst boxers can sneak in a lucky punch occasionally.
- Stay focused and keep a positive attitude. Stay relaxed and change the tempo when you sense your partner is getting frustrated or tired.
- After the sparring session, debrief quickly with your partner. Identify any fouls he/she committed. Let him/her know two or three things that you saw that need to be improved. Tell him/her three things he/she did well in the sparring session.

The easiest way to work with a novice boxer is to have definite ideas about what you want to accomplish in the ring. Do you want to work on your defensive skills? Does your partner need to work on footwork, throwing more punches, or being aggressive? Your goals should complement each other. For example, if you work on defense, your partner will work on offense. Consider the specific skills you want to work on, and tell your partner the plan before you step into the ring.

Table 4.2 provides examples of directives and exercises you might use when sparring with a novice boxer.

Gaining the Strategic Advantage

Table 4.2
Working with the Novice Boxer

Goals	Sparring Exercise
You work on slipping/sliding and The novice works on throwing straight punches with good form	Have your partner throw a lot of 1s and 2s to your head; only throw back at your partner if he/she is getting lazy, or is dropping his/her hands
You work on getting out of corners and The novice works on being aggressive, controlling the ring, and capitalizing on a boxer in the corner	Have your partner be aggressive in the ring and pin you in the corners with all punches to both the head and body; only throw back at your partner if her/his form is getting sloppy
You work on all defensive moves and The novice works on being aggressive and throwing a lot of punches	Have your partner work on all offensive moves, including all punches to both the head and body; only throw back at your partner if his/her form is getting sloppy or lazy
You work on sidestepping (angles) and The novice works on throwing a lot of punches	Have your partner work on all offensive punches, and staying busy in the ring; only throw back at your partner if he/she is not aggressive
You work on infighting and/or counterpunching and The novice works on defensive moves and counters	Have your partner work the jab to initiate an infighting situation; throw punches that counter your partner but take the edge off your punches; work your inside defensive moves to make the counters work
You work on moving around the ring and staying light on your feet and The novice works on getting in range and cutting off the ring	Have your partner be aggressive in the ring and try to connect with the jab; do not throw any punches, but rather attempt to evade your opponent only using your footwork

Sparring with Boxers Who Are Better or Stronger Than You

As mentioned in the previous essay, the value of sparring lies in its potential to hone your boxing skills. If you cannot find a sparring partner who is evenly matched with you, then ask a more advanced boxer in your gym if they would be interested in working with you in some working sparring sessions. Most boxers will be flattered that you believe you can learn something from them.

When you spar someone considerably better or stronger than you, make sure the skilled person understands your sparring philosophy and goals for the sparring session. Gym coaches are responsible for overseeing sparring sessions. However, in some gyms there are not enough coaches to watch all exercises and give instruction to every boxer at all times. If you must broker a sparring session on your own, then be very specific about what you want to accomplish in the ring. You should choose a partner whom you have seen spar successfully with other people, and who has the following five qualities:

1. The better boxer should understand common boxing techniques and be able to follow directions. Remember that you will be asking specific things of your sparring partner, therefore look for someone who understands simple instructions before the drill begins.
2. The better boxer must be able to maintain control at all times. As the novice, or weaker, boxer you are especially vulnerable to being hit, becoming tired, and/or getting hurt.
3. The better boxer must look relaxed in the ring. If your potential partner looks timid and/or fearful, then he/she will not be able to control him/herself, and may try to punish or retaliate when hit.
4. The better boxer should be in good shape. If your potential partner can spar four or five rounds without getting too tired, he/she will be able to sustain a working session with you for two or three rounds, even after they have sparred someone else.
5. The better boxer should box cleanly, so you can practice good form.

Sparring with partners who are better and/or stronger than you can elevate your intensity, focus, and stamina in practices. Strong partners can be valuable teachers in the ring.

Chapter Five
Keys to Successful Competition

Competition: Boxing Styles

The ability to defeat your opponent is, in part, dependent upon your ability to anticipate what he or she will do against you in competition. You will find that you will get better at reading your opponent's boxing style as you accumulate experience in the ring. Coaches and trainers use style patterns to help boxers take advantage of their strengths and avoid circumstances that will expose any weaknesses. Most of your opponents will develop style patterns in the ring. If you are mentally prepared to counter any of the particular styles listed here, then you will be ready to capitalize on your opponent's weaknesses in the ring and increase your ability to dominate each round of competition.

Below are some hints for boxing seven different kinds of opponents: short opponents, tall opponents, left-handers, wild boxers, crouchers, boxers, and sluggers. Read the following hints keeping in mind that boxers do not always perform predictably. Additionally, most of your opponents are aware of what you have been told about their perceived strengths and weaknesses, so boxers will sometimes change strategies and/or styles from time to time. Lastly, good boxers may switch styles in the middle of a bout in hopes of confusing you. Be prepared to alter your strategy in the middle of a bout, if you read a different style used by your opponent.

You can assess another boxer's style while they compete or spar against someone else, exercise on focus mitts, and shadowbox. Watch for telltale combinations and movement patterns in any or all of these situations in order to identify what kind of style your opponent is most likely to use in the ring. Assessing a boxing style is a skill, so ask a coach or another boxer to help you correctly identify the style of your potential opponents.

Identify your own style, too, so you know the strategies the opposition will likely employ against you in a bout. Box in the style in which you are most comfortable, but consider using elements of other styles sometimes to avoid boxing predictably.

**Develop your critical eye
by becoming a student of the sport.**

Boxing a Shorter Opponent

Do not assume you have an advantage just because you are taller than your opponent: you cannot afford to take an opponent lightly. Never underestimate any opponent, no matter his/her size or perceived strength or speed. If you are taller, then you can expect your opponent will try to move to the inside, work the body, and duck under your punches. Knowing this, you should be prepared with the following strategies:

Keep your distance. If your opponent wants you close, then keep away. Stay out of the boxing zone where he/she can sneak in and smother your punches. In close range you won't be able to snap your punches as well as your shorter opponent.

Keep your opponent on the end of your punches and work the jab. Maintaining adequate distance will help you keep your target at the end of your punches where the snap is effective. Pick apart a shorter boxer—by using your jab—if he/she is waiting for a chance to get inside on you. Be patient, and compel your opponent to keep working to get within striking distance.

Use the whole ring. Maintain proper distance by utilizing all of the ring. You may have longer legs than your opponent, thus you may not expend as much energy as he/she would trying to keep up with you. Make your opponent work to engage you.

Stay out of the corners. Don't get trapped in the corners where your opponent can easily force you to one side or the other. If you do get trapped, remember not to head hunt in an effort to get out. Your opponent's body may be lower than yours, but he/she may move his/her head more easily to slip punches and make you miss.

Be prepared to look for your opponent. If your opposition uses the duck, he/she will probably step to the side with the duck in order to keep you looking for him/her. Knowing this, be prepared to cover and sidestep into neutral territory in order to re-establish your distance and use your jab effectively.

Take a half-step back. If an opponent has a shorter reach, he/she will have shorter punches, therefore you can effectively use the half-step back. Look for opportunities to use your momentum to move forward again.

Keep your chin down. Taller boxers often forget they still need to keep their chin down against someone smaller. The chin is vulnerable and should always be protected, no matter the size or style of your opponent.

Anyone can get caught by a lucky punch. Be prepared.

Keep your punches—especially the jab—crisp and clean. Taller boxers often get lazy with their punches, throwing them lackadaisically or forgetting to rotate the shoulder with the extended arm.

Gauge the style of your opponent. Though he/she may be smaller, check for the style your opponent incorporates. Box your opponent's style, not just their size.

Boxing a Taller Opponent

Being shorter than your opponent doesn't have to put you at a disadvantage—if you plan ahead and execute your strategy correctly. The following are several points to keep in mind when boxing a taller opponent.

Do not "head hunt." Since your opponent's head is higher than yours you will pop out of your stance if you try to always reach to the head. This may cause you to swing wildly and lunge in, which will leave you vulnerable. You may also have a tendency to bring your chin up when you go to the head which may expose your jaw or neck.

Counterpunch your way inside. Your opponent will likely have been told to use the jab against you. Turn the tables by expecting it. Draw the lead jab and slip your way inside to attack the body.

Work the body. Most boxers forget that working the body is a central component to boxing. Hitting the body is effective. If you tire someone's body, he/she will slow down. This will force him/her to overprotect the area and will leave the head vulnerable to attack. Clean body blows can score as well as head shots.

Your opponent will expect you to work the body. Taller opponents will be prepared for you to move in low. To counter this, create openings using the feint, jab, hook, and sidestep. Then duck inside for the body attack.

Be smart and keep moving. When you are low you are vulnerable to punches coming from above. Counter this by utilizing the feint and by changing up your combinations. Don't just plow your way into the body and stay there. Work downstairs, then upstairs, and move. Change your positioning, your punches, your target, and your intensity.

Don't get trapped in the corners. While it is dangerous for any boxer to back him/herself into corners, it is especially dangerous for the shorter opponent. Referees will be watching closely in these situations—do not give the referee an excuse to stop the bout. You can get out of a corner by timing a move or punching your way out. Be patient and read what your opponent is throwing. Additionally, many boxers throw big shots when they get someone in the corner—their punches become slower and heavy. Use this to your advantage by turning your punches up the middle with uppercuts to the head and body. Keep everything in tight so that you "thread a needle" with your counter shots.

Points win matches. Even if you feel like your opponent hits you harder, you can win the bout. Clean touches count—not sloppy ones. A scoring blow must not be blocked, must connect with the knuckle of the glove, and it must be thrown with the weight of the body or shoulder behind it. Take your time and throw correct punches. Work defensive moves off your offense and your offense off your defense.

The bigger they are the harder they fall. Bigger opponents will likely be slower than you, but they will also cover more ground because they have longer legs. Make sure you move side to side while ducking under their arms. Use the "V-step in-and-out" technique of movement so your opponent has to constantly look for you. Move around your opponent, especially to the jab side, away from his/her power. Do *not* stand in front of your opponent—you become a target if you stay in front and try to "slug it out."

Boxing a Left-Hander if You Are a Right-Handed Boxer

Most left-handed boxers have the advantage over right-handers simply because there are fewer lefties, so most right-handers don't get to practice against them. Conversely, most left-handers get lots of practice against right-handers. As a result, right-handers are often frustrated when they face a left-handed opponent. Though left-handers can have a variety of boxing styles, there are some general rules that may help you face a left-handed boxer.

Keep your foot to the outside of your opponent's lead foot. From this position, you will be better able to control the pace and space of the ring and you will stay away from your opponent's strong side, his/her left hand. Don't panic if your foot is stepped on or you step on your opponent's foot: continue to keep your guard up. Your opponent may even step on your foot purposefully, so expect it.

Change leads. Throw a lead right or a hook in order to pierce the left-hander's defense. The lead right hand and lead hook are *not* power shots. These punches should be thrown quickly. Throw either lead from a relaxed position so your opponent doesn't have a chance to read it. Throw alternate leads to both the head and body.

Catch jabs with your left hand. Unlike your right-handed opponents, lefties will shoot the jab in a way that is easier to catch with your left hand. By catching with the left you have freed up the right. Throw the right to the body or the head after a catch.

Circle to your left. Keep away from your opponent's power by circling away from it. And watch for them to throw the right hook.

Make the southpaw come to you. Don't always lead. Let your opponent expose his/her vulnerabilities first, sometimes. Utilize the side step (to the left, mostly) in order to avoid jabs.

Take angles. Though you should always work on taking angles against all opponents, it is especially important when boxing unorthodox boxers. Keep them looking for you and pick them apart by moving on the attack.

Watch for the switch between the left and right-handed stance. Most left-handed boxers like to change up their stance to throw off their opponents. Stay relaxed and be prepared for them to switch.

Be smart and stay patient. Use the feint to draw your opponent into your offense so you can capitalize on telegraphed or badly thrown punches. Watch the rest of your opponent's style, too. Does he or she like to box, slug, or overextend? Be patient in the ring. For the inexperienced, boxing left-handers can be especially challenging. Don't panic if you misread them on occasion.

Ready your hook. One of the most effective weapons against a lefty is the right-hander's left hook. Be ready to throw it, but remember the hook is a relatively slow punch, so use it appropriately.

Slide punch. Catch with the left hand and shoot the jab over the top of your catch—it's a quick punch your opponent won't expect.

Control the pace of each round, and the space of the ring, to gain control of the bout.

Boxing a Wild Fighter

Inexperienced, lazy, or tired boxers are awkward and out of control. Wild boxers are scared, and in their haste they often leave themselves open. However, boxing a wild opponent is a danger to you because they are unpredictable, and may score a lucky punch.

A few pointers for boxing someone who is wild:

Stay calm. Your opponent is scared and inexperienced. You will likely perform badly if you get caught up in trying to fight wildly. Keep true to your style and stay calm as he/she pushes, holds, wrestles, slaps, and posts on you. Your opponent will be called for fouls. Show good sportsmanship by accepting apologies for fouling. Keep your cool and capitalize on your opponent's mistakes.

Follow up on haymaker misses. The wild fighter wants to knock you out. Therefore, he/she will throw haymakers, or heavy-handed desperation shots to the head. Be alert. Use the half-step back or the duck to make the wild fighter miss, then follow up with your own counters.

Move around a lot. The wild boxer usually takes lunging steps, sometimes running to the opponent. Stay in good boxing position, on your toes, and move all around the ring to prevent your opponent from getting set.

Use the duck and side step. Wild boxers usually rush forward in an effort to score a blow. The side step will remove you from the path of their fists (especially if you duck occasionally) and still keep you in good position to score as they lunge by you. Use a short cross to the body, a hook, or uppercut. Wild boxers often take looping shots to your head, so be prepared to duck and move. Again, stay in range so you can counter their missed shots.

Throw straight blows, and keep your chin down. Throw straight punches to beat looping punches. Maintain correct form whenever you throw so that you do not leave yourself open to lucky shots your opponent may sneak in. Likewise, keep your chin down.

Follow up on all scoring blows. Be sure to follow up scoring blows with a barrage of punches. Overwhelming your opponent may draw them into a vulnerable position.

Use multiple jabs. Most wild fighters cannot throw punches while moving backwards. By throwing multiple stiff jabs, you can keep your opponent away from you and simultaneously stay out of their range.

Use feints. Inexperienced and wild boxers will be confused by feints.

Keys to Successful Competition

Use feints somewhat sparingly, though, so as not to become predictable.

Don't panic if you get hit with a lucky shot. Every boxer has the potential to score on you. Part of being a good boxer is anticipating what your opponent will throw. Sometimes you will misread your opponent. If you become obsessed with the few blows they score on you, more will surely follow. Being a good boxer means keeping your focus, even when you get hit or when you know your opponent scored a point.

Boxing a Croucher

A croucher is a boxer who lowers his/her head and bends the legs so that he/she is low and literally in a "crouched over" position. The croucher generally throws short punches, but will come out of their couched position to land hard punches. Crouchers like to keep their distance, but will engage in infighting if the opportunity arises.

Stop the advance by throwing a straight 1-2 to the chin. Step in with these punches. The croucher may be stopped in his/her tracks, thus ending the attack.

Sidestep and counter. The croucher isn't light on his/her feet. The side step will keep the croucher looking for you and put you in position to throw the jab and cross from an angle that will be more likely to score.

Throw uppercuts. Crouchers often bend at the waist, "tipping their hat" to you. When this is the case, you have a perfect target for an uppercut.

Take advantage of holds. The croucher may attempt to hold (or clinch) in order to avoid being hit. When your opponent attempts to hold, a sharp movement downward or backwards may break the hold, and give you momentum with which to immediately counter.

Use multiple jabs. Throw multiple jabs to keep crouchers away from you and out of range. Circle as you jab in order to keep your opponent looking for you.

Follow up on all scoring blows. A croucher may give up when you score on him/her, so always be sure to follow up scoring blows with even more punches. If he/she retreats by crouching even more, most referees will issue a warning to him/her for being passive.

Boxing a Boxer

The boxer is usually calm, cool, and collected. The boxer likes to move a lot (including backwards), throw the jab, and counterpunch. Generally, boxers do not like to be hit. They will be patient in the ring and also will work various defenses in order to score the most clean blows. The boxer has a broad range of punches at his or her disposal, though most often he or she will throw the jab or a straight cross. Generally, the boxer will box in a calculated manner, showing a variety of punches, angles, and defensive tactics. This is the most common style in international bouts, such as the Olympic Games.

When you encounter a boxer, remember to do the following:

Don't stand upright. A boxer wants to put you on the end of his/her punches. The jab will be effective against you if you walk into it or if you stay up so high that you are stopped by it. Bending your legs and moving your head will make your opponent miss and will take the power off of his/her jabs.

Force the action continuously. Make the boxer move backwards and stay on guard rather than on the offensive. Be prepared for counters. Use the feint so he/she covers up one area by sacrificing another. Use a whirlwind attack in order to keep your opponent off balance.

Time a cross to the chin. Some boxers are afraid of big hitters. Be a big hitter some of the time. Try to time a cross to the chin in order to sting the boxer, and make him/her cover in defense. Once the head is covered, the body is open to attack.

Have counters ready to go. The boxer will jab continuously, so have your counters ready. Slip to the inside or outside guard position and work the body, then the head. Use the draw to counter his/her counters.

Make your opponent lead on occasion. If the boxer is a counterpuncher, make him/her lead some of the time. If your opponent refuses to lead, try to force him/her into a lead by feinting a lead of your own, or by drawing.

Be ready to catch the jab. The boxer loves to jab. Have your right hand up (if you are right-handed) and ready to catch jabs. Change up your reaction to the jab (catch, slip, duck, and move) so the boxer can't read any patterns in your style.

Stay under control. The boxer often waits for you to make a mistake. Don't give your opponent what he/she wants simply because you are impatient. Keep your balance during combinations to

Keys to Successful Competition

minimize the effect of a miss. Expect to miss often, because good boxers usually evade punches well.

Focus on scoring blows. Don't waste your energy by trying to make contact with a boxer who is out of range and/or moves well in the ring. Use the jab to stop your opponent's movement or to create openings when your opponent tries to counter and/or evade your punches. Straight punches will score cleanly and more quickly than looping punches, such as the hook.

Boxing a Slugger

Sluggers generally move straight forward and attack their opposition with great force. Most sluggers are hard hitters, because they use forward momentum to propel their punches. Trying to hit someone hard usually leaves openings for counterattacks, but most sluggers will happily trade getting hit for a chance to hit their opponents.

When engaged with a slugger, remember the following:

Keep moving. A slugger generally has to get set in order to land hard punches. If the target (that's you) is constantly moving, the slugger can't get set. Let the slugger chase you as you score with a long-range jab.

Attack suddenly. When your opponent cannot get set for offense, he/she likely will not be prepared to defend, either. Attack quickly and then move at an angle in order to score again. Moving away at an angle will keep the slugger from hunting you down by simply taking a few steps forward. Keep your opponent guessing.

Use multiple jabs. Throwing multiple jabs will keep the slugger away from you and will keep you out of his/her range. Circle the slugger as you jab in order to keep him/her looking for you, so your opponent never gets his/her feet settled.

Don't slug. Do not stand toe-to-toe with sluggers. They want (and need) for you to stay within reach, so don't do it. Move out quickly after you score blows. Keep circling to the right (if the slugger is right-handed) to stay away from the slugger's strong side.

Use the uppercut against the jab. Sluggers are notorious for overextending their jab because they want to hurry and deliver the power punch. Use a quick dip and uppercut to the chin against an overextended jab. This will stop your opponent's momentum and will likely sting, even if it is not thrown with power. Practice this skill in the gym before you try it in the ring.

Use no-look, overhand crosses. A slugger usually will drop his/her defensive glove when he/she attacks because he/she is so excited about the attack. This leaves your opponent open for a quick overhand hook (when he/she throws a jab) or quick overhand cross (when he/she is throwing a cross). This is especially useful when you find yourself against the ropes or in the corner against a slugger. Stay patient and time your no-look punches.

Close the gap on your opponent's attack. If your opponent happens to move in range to attack, move into him/her so that you close any gap that he/she can use to hit you. If you are too close to your opponent, then he/she won't have enough room to hit you. Cover up well when using this strategy.

Feint. Someone who overextends is also susceptible to the feint. Draw in your opponent, sidestep, and land any combination of punches as he/she moves past you.

Never underestimate an opponent.

Boxing Specifically for Judges (Part I): Traditional and Computerized Scoring Systems

The winner of an amateur bout is determined by trained judges who count the number of scoring blows thrown by each boxer. A scoring blow is identified with the following five (5) standard criteria:
1. must be thrown with the weight of the body or shoulder
2. must connect with the knuckle-surface of the glove
3. must connect with the opponent in a legal scoring area (the front or sides of the head and/or body above the opponent's beltline)
4. may not be picked, parried, or blocked by the opponent
5. must connect while not infringing a rule

This stringent criteria is difficult to meet, and thus typically results in boxing matches with low scores. All amateur bouts end by one of the following determinations:
1. points (calculated by the number of scoring blows landed)
2. RSC (referee stops the contest)
3. RSCH (referee stops the contest because of a head blow)
4. retirement (a boxer doesn't return to the match after a rest interval, or a coach stops the match)
5. disqualification (the referee stops the bout because one boxer is infringing on the rules to an extreme, or after the accumulation of three warnings)
6. walkover (if the opponent doesn't enter the ring when the bout is scheduled to begin)
7. no contest (when extraneous circumstances, such as a broken ring, power outages, etc. prevents the match from occuring)
8. draw (when judges vote for a "tie")

In the case of points, the most common result of contests, the majority of the three or five judges agree on a winner based on their tally of points that each boxer earned during the bout. The remainder of this essay explains the ways points are scored in both traditional (also known as "paper scoring") and computerized scoring (also known as "electronic scoring").

Traditional Scoring

In traditional scoring, each judge watches each round and determines how many scoring blows one boxer landed over the other. At the end of

Judge's Score Card

Date _____
Weight Class _____   Bout Number _____

Red Corner				Blue Corner	
Name _____				Name _____	
Representing _____				Representing _____	
Remarks	Points	Round	Points	Remarks	
		1			
		2			
		3			
		4			
		Total			

I award the bout to _____

Referee _____
Name   Signature of Judge

Points	Referee Stopped Contest		Disqualified	Retirement	No Contest	Walkover
	RSC	RSCH				

Typical judge's scorecard for amateur boxing

the round, each judge writes down his/her score on his/her official scorecard. The winner of the round automatically receives 20 points (this system is also called a "20-point must system"). The loser of the round receives one point less for every three scoring blows landed against him/her. Every scoring blow counts as one-third of a point, regardless of how hard it was thrown or even if it resulted in a standing-eight count or knockdown.

For example, if the red corner landed nine scoring blows more than the blue corner, the official score would be 20 (red) to 17 (blue). The points awarded at the end of a round may be rounded up in the case of two scoring blows thrown (called the "two-thirds rule"), so a boxer who scored two blows over the opponent would win the round 20 to 19. If both boxers have scored the same number of blows or are only separated by one scoring blow, then the round would be scored 20 to 20.

If a boxer infringes on a rule, the referee may stop the action and issue a "caution" to that boxer by demonstrating the infraction quickly to the offender. If a boxer is cautioned three times for the same infraction, or it appears as though the boxer is breaking a rule intentionally, then the referee may issue a warning.

When a referee issues a warning in traditional scoring, one point is deducted from that boxer's round score. Therefore, a boxer who lost the round 19 to 20 and also had a point taken away would have a total round score of 18 to 20. If a boxer won the round 20 to 19, but was warned, then the round would be scored 20 to 20, since the 20-point must rule ensures at least one boxer must score 20 points in the round. Round scores are summed at the completion of the bout.

If both boxers have scored the same number of total points, then the judge awards the bout to the boxer believed to be the better boxer, as indicated by ring generalship, effective aggression, and style (including defense). The judge notes this in the "remarks" column of his or her scorecard. The boxer who was selected as winning on all (unanimous) or the majority (split decision) of the judges' scorecards is declared the winner.

TACTICS TO USE WITH TRADITIONAL SCORING

Be aggressive. Take control of the bout so you appear to dominate your opponent. If you give your opponent a standing-eight count, it will not add points to your score, but it may stick in the mind of the judges and the referee as a sign that you outclass your opponent.

Use the corners to your advantage. Remember that the judges sit on opposite sides from each other and may not be able to see all punches that you throw; however, if you back your opponent into a corner, the judges may interpret you as the aggressor.

Be first with punches. Indicate aggressiveness to the judges in order to capitalize the subjective nature of traditional scoring.

Use defense to evade or deflect punches. This prevents your opponent's punches from being counted as scoring blows by the judges. Good defense also shows that you have "style" in the ring, and that you have sound technique and a command of boxing skills.

Win the first rounds. If you are ahead in the first rounds, your opponent will have difficulty catching up in the later ones.

Computerized Scoring

Most international shows and tournaments use computerized scoring to promote fair decisions for boxers. The computerized system is designed to remove some of the subjective elements of amateur judging and to identify any bias among judges. Computerized scoring has several advantages, including:

1. Judges no longer have to keep mental count of scoring blows.

2. Judges are more likely to record scoring blows. In paper judging it is easy to lose count and to base the winner on subjective criteria at the end of the round.

Judge sitting ringside with computer keypad.

3. The actions of judges are recorded on the computer and can be analyzed for bias toward a boxer or a team, or even to determine whether a judge is unskilled or tired.

4. The winner of a bout is determined instantly as the bout ends.

5. Bouts are cleaner and safer since boxers know they will only win if they score cleanly, as judges will not factor in subjective criteria.

6. Boxers are less likely to commit fouls since their opponent is rewarded two points for a warning.

How computerized scoring works

Each ringside judge uses a keypad to record every scoring blow he/she witnesses. The keypad contains four buttons: red and blue buttons record scoring blows for each boxer, and two "W" keys record warnings for each boxer. The keypads are connected to a computer where the time that each judge presses a button is recorded. When a judge presses a button to record a scoring blow for either boxer, that judge opens a one-second window. If one (in the case of three judges being used) or two (in the case of five judges being used) other judges also press the scoring button for the same boxer within the one-second window, then the computer awards one point to that boxer (called an "accepted score"). The computer keeps a running score of unaccepted and accepted points recorded for each judge. At the end of a bout the accepted score points are totaled, and the winner is named as the boxer with the most accepted scoring blows.

If the accepted score for each boxer is the same (a tie), then the computer tallies the individual judge's scores (accepted and unaccepted points), removes the highest and lowest scores for both boxers, and these "raw punches" are

Computer keypad

used to declare the winner. If the boxers are still tied (an unusual occurrence), each judge is asked to press the score button for the boxer he or she deems as the winner, based on subjective criteria such as ring generalship.

When a referee warns a boxer for a foul, each judge presses that boxer's "W" button. Two points are then awarded to the accepted score of the warned boxer's opponent (the boxer on whom the foul was committed). If a judge disagrees with the warning, he or she may choose not to press the "W" button. A majority of judges must agree on the warning in order for the points to be awarded to the accepted score.

Throughout the entire bout, a computer technician (always a certified official) monitors the computer to make sure the scoring system is working properly. If a boxer scores a great deal more points over an opponent, the jury (as notified by the computer technician) *may* stop the bout and declare the winner immediately (the number of points is based on the boxers' classification). At the end of the bout, printouts are given to the jury and to the chief of officials to make sure that judging was fair and accurate.

Finally, where computerized scoring is used, three judges are typically keeping score on paper. This is a redundant system so that if the computer malfunctions, paper scores can be used to declare the winner.

TACTICS TO USE WITH COMPUTERIZED SCORING

Throw punches. Judges will only count scoring blows that meet the scoring blow criteria. Therefore the boxers must throw scoring punches in order to score points.

Use defense. If you can deflect or avoid a scoring blow, then your opponent has not met the criteria and will not earn points.

Do not fall behind. Since points are cumulative over the three or four rounds, a boxer can lose the first two or three rounds but still win the bout if he/she has a strong last round.

Box cleanly. A warning costs a boxer two points added to the opponent's accepted score. In some bouts, recovering from a deficit of this kind can be difficult.

Don't waste your energy on careless punches. If your punches are inaccurate or don't meet the scoring blow criteria, then judges will not count them as scoring blows.

Don't go toe-to-toe with your opponent. Trading close-range punches, even if done in the center of the ring, will be difficult to see. Make infighting clean so your scoring blows can be easily counted by judges.

Maintain your lead through the entire bout. Use defense effectively, but don't forget to continue scoring.

If you are behind, focus on landing clean scoring blows. Be the first to score and the last to score when engaged with your opponent.

Don't look for the knockout punch. You can get behind quickly on points if you wait for the perfect opportunity to throw your knockout punch.

Throw body punches. If they are seen, they will be counted. Throwing body punches often opens your opponent for a clean blow to the head, and/or causes him/her to make mistakes.

Use combinations. Combinations create openings. A combinations will also increase the possibility of judges recording a scoring blow within a one-second window—even if each saw a different scoring punch.

Boxing Specifically for Judges (Part II): Judges' Positions at Ringside

Once you can box comfortably and confidently in the ring and understand the basic strategies for successful boxing, you can box specifically for the positioning of the ringside judges. In all amateur boxing, bouts will be scored either by three or five judges. Professional boxing uses two or three judges at ringside (some professional shows use the referee as a third judge). The illustrations and strategies shown below are based on the five-part amateur judging criteria.

The ring diagrams show typical ring set-ups using three (Figure 5.1) and five (Figure 5.2) judges. However, the officials or event organizers may slightly alter the placement of boxer corners and/or judges. At all times, judges sit at ringside, across from each other. When five judges are used, two judges will sit near each other on one side of the ring.

Generally, some areas of the ring afford greater visibility for judges than others. Since judges must see the punch and target clearly in order to count it as a scoring blow, they must have a large viewing area. The center of the ring always affords the greatest visibility while the boxers are moving and vying for position. The center of the ring is marked with a circle in Figures 5.1 and 5.2. Placing your back to a judge virtually guarantees your scoring blows will not be counted by that judge since he/she will not be able to tell how and where your punches land. If you are overwhelmed by an opponent, or are tired, you may want to move

Keys to Successful Competition

into a "blind area" of the ring.

Maximum and minimum visibility in the ring depends on placing yourself in a position so a majority or a minority of ringside judges can view your actions. The number of judges at ringside influences the positions that afford the greatest and least amount of visibility.

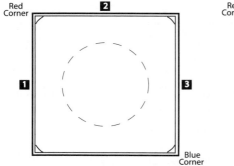

Figure 5.1: Three judges at ringside.

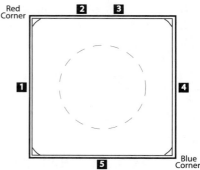

Figure 5.2: Five judges at ringside.

Three Judges

When boxing in the center of the ring, try to position yourself so your side (especially your "open" side) is visible to two judges. In Figure 5.3, the boxers in the center of the ring have maximum exposure because both of their sides can be viewed by judges one and three. The boxers nearing the two corners are also visible to two of the judges, sitting adjacent to eah other.

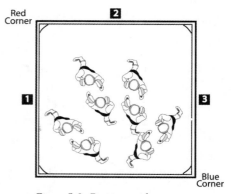

Figure 5.3: Positions with maximum visibility for three judges.

If you are able to control your opponent, and wish to back him/her into a corner, choose a corner in which two of the three judges can witness the scoring blows you land. The other judge will only have a view of your back, and therefore not be able to award any points. Figure 5.4 shows the two corners of the ring that provide maximum exposure to judges. Boxing in the red corner will allow a good view by judges one and two, while boxing in the neutral corner between judges two and three gives those two judges an adequate view to count scoring blows.

If you are overwhelmed by an opponent, you will want to position yourself in the ring so the judges are less likely to award points to your opponent. Figure 5.5 shows the best corners in which to take a rest or "hide" from judges would be the blue corner and the nearest neutral corner, since only one judge will have a view of your opponent's scoring blows. Another blind zone for the majority of judges would be in the middle of the ring where your side is facing only judge two, since judges one and three will have a view of your back or your opponent's back.

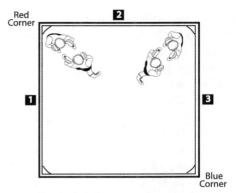

Figure 5.4: Corners with maximum visibility for three judges.

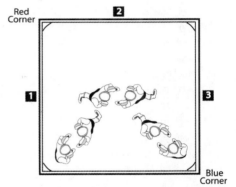

Figure 5.5: Areas of the ring with minimum visibility for three judges.

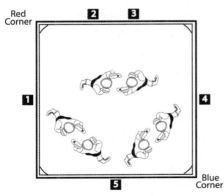

Figure 5.6: Positions with maximum visibility for five judges.

Five Judges

In the case of five judges, maximum visibility can be attained by boxing in the middle of the ring or at an angle where at least three of the five judges have view of your punches. Figure 5.6 shows that the middle of the ring (with each boxer facing judge one or four), or angles near the blue corner and neutral corner between judges five and one, are within view of

Keys to Successful Competition

the majority of judges.

The red corner and neutral corner between judges three and four can both be used to your advantage, since these corners provide an ample view of your punches. Figure 5.7 illustrates that moving your opponent into the corners nearest the side with two judges virtually guarantees your punches will be visible to three of the five judges at ringside.

If you want to be out of view from the majority of judges, box in the blue corner, or in the neutral corner between judges one and five. As Figure 5.8 shows, these corners can really only be viewed by two judges, and therefore punches are not likely to be scored by others. If you find yourself in the middle of the ring, but want to hide from view, turn so that both you and your opponent have your backs to judges five, two, and three.

Regardless of the number of officials judging you bout, or whether they use traditional or computer scoring, use to your advantage your knowledge of these variables. Always pay careful attention to the judges' position and be concious of how you use the ring space.

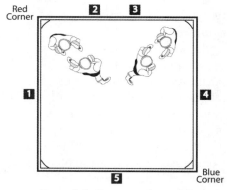

Figure 5.7: Corners with maximum visibility for five judges.

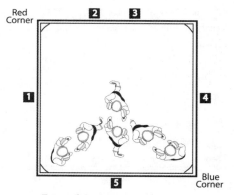

Figure 5.8: Corners with minimum visibility for five judges.

Managing Ring Variables: Dimensions and Flooring Materials

Though amateur and professional boxing is sanctioned by governing bodies that enforce regulations regarding competition rings, you will find that all rings are different. Rings differ in their dimensions (measured from the inside of one side of ropes to the inside of the opposite side), and in the type of padding and canvas that covers the floor of the ring. Dimension and surface can greatly affect the strategy of you or your opponent, so you should be prepared to box in any type of ring.

The size of an amateur boxing ring must be 16, 18, or 20 feet inside the ropes. Professional rings can be even smaller, and are determined by the regulations of independent governing bodies.

The surface covering a ring's floor can be made of canvas (the most popular) or vinyl. Vinyl surfaces are easier to keep clean since they can be washed with a mop; however, they can become slick when they get wet with sweat or especially in the corners from water used during the rest intervals. Also, the amount and type of padding used under the covering (between the canvas and the wood subfloor) will influence your ability to move. If the padding is thin, the surface will be firm and you can move effortlessly and quickly, thus it is typically referred to as a "fast ring." A ring with soft or thick padding is known as a "slow ring," since you "sink" into the material and must work harder to move around.

Brawlers will benefit from small or soft rings and are especially advantaged in rings that are both small *and* soft. A small ring (16 feet or less) benefits a slow boxer, or a boxer who likes to brawl, since the opponent doesn't have much space in which to move away. Many professional shows use a small ring in order to "force" the action between the pugilists. Slow rings are difficult to move in, therefore brawlers can more easily catch up with boxers who would otherwise prefer to move around the entire ring in an effort to avoid the brawler's punches.

In contrast, a large ring (20 feet) benefits the boxer who is in constant motion, takes angles, and moves in and out of boxing range. Boxers who use the space of a large ring can evade punches and stay away from sluggers. Fast rings benefit quick-moving boxers, too, since the firm surface provides little resistance to quick movements.

Keys to Successful Competition

Often, boxers or brawlers will find themselves in a ring that is detrimental to their own strategy. If you are a boxer, and find yourself in a small or soft ring, you can do the following to minimize the effect of the ring on your style:
- Pick up your feet when you move.
- Feint to draw your opponent into planting him/herself for the punch.
- Back your opponent into a corner with the stiff jab: getting out of the corner or the ropes in a slow ring will be difficult for him/her.
- Stay in the middle of the ring so you aren't forced into corners.
- Take angles around your opponent on defense (don't move straight backward).
- Use combinations; don't throw one punch at a time.

If you are a slugger, and find yourself in a large or fast ring, you can do the following:
- Cut off the ring and don't allow the opponent to move to the center.
- Use the jab to close the distance between you and your opponent.
- Use the feint to see which direction your opponent is moving (so you can cut off his/her movement).
- Stay in the middle of the ring so your opponent is forced to expend more energy as he/she moves around you.

Every ring is different, and you will rarely compete in a ring you view as perfect. Be prepared to box in any type of ring by practicing on different surfaces and by being technically sound in your training. If you are confident in your training, the type of ring won't be a major factor in your success.

Table 5.1
The Effects of Ring Size and Type

Ring size		less than 16'	16'	18'	20'	22'
Ring type	Hard	brawler		boxer	boxer	boxer
	Firm	brawler		boxer	boxer	boxer
	Medium	brawler	brawler		boxer	boxer
	Semi-soft	brawler	brawler	brawler		boxer
	Soft	brawler	brawler	brawler	brawler	

What to Expect When You Box in Amateur Boxing Shows

In order to prepare yourself for competing in amateur boxing shows, use these lists as a reference. Ask your coach about expectations for your participation in amateur boxing events.

Checklist of Items You Need to Pack for Bouts

- ❒ Your (valid) passbook*
- ❒ Your driver's license (or another picture ID)
- ❒ Regulation headgear*
- ❒ Groin protector*
- ❒ Properly fitted mouthpiece
- ❒ Velpeau or gauze for wrapping hands*
- ❒ Small towel for the ring*
- ❒ Boxing top* (sleeveless, like a tank top; long enough to tuck into your trunks — color must contrast with the trunks' waistband)
- ❒ Trunks/shorts* (waist band must be a different color than the shirt)
- ❒ Shoes (boxing or tennis-type shoes; no running shoes) and socks
- ❒ Water bottle

Standard Procedures

All boxers must have their weight checked by a weigh official. Same-sex weigh-ins are mandatory. After your weight is checked, you will be required to see the ringside physician. The physician may check your blood pressure, pulse, pupils, and soreness in your hands and face. Be honest with the physician at all times, alerting him/her to illnesses, situational medical conditions (like allergies), or previous injuries (if you were recently knocked out in practice, or if you are suffering from headaches, etc.). When you are finished with your weigh-in and physical, you may begin to prepare for your bout.

The clerk will make matches and assign an order to the event card. This card will be posted. Find your name and the time when you are to participate.

Prepare yourself by wrapping your hands, for example, keeping in mind that your coach will have to tend to all boxers in your club. Warm up by following your coach's instructions, which may include jumping rope, shadowboxing, and/or hitting focus mitts. At most events

*These items may be provided by your coach.

Keys to Successful Competition

you can get your competition gloves on as early as three bouts before your own.

You will box three or four rounds of one to two minutes in length, depending upon your classification (based on your age and level of experience). The weight of your gloves depends on your weight class.*

Remember

- In amateur boxing, points win matches.
- Accuracy and *number of punches landed* count for points.
- If the score is tied, judges will also score on *"ring generalship"*: your ability to control the bout with defense, efficient offense, your overall style, and general aggressiveness.
- Always listen to the referee. During a round you will hear only three commands: "stop," "box," and "break." If told to break, you must disengage and take one full step backwards with each foot before continuing the action. If told to "stop," disengage immediately and look at the referee for instructions. After a "stop," action will resume only after the referee gives the command to "box."
- Do *not* touch gloves with your opponent during the bout (after the sound of the first bell). If you want to apologize for a foul, bow quickly to your opponent from a safe distance.
- If you are told to go to the neutral corner, go there and face the middle of the ring. Watch the referee for further instructions.
- If you are given a standing-eight count, stay calm. The referee will count all the way to eight without stopping. If you want to continue the bout, raise your hands in boxing position (at the count of 3 or 4) to signal to the referee that you want to continue.

Reminders of What to Do After Your Bout

- Shake hands (touch gloves) with your opponent after the bout.
- Shake hands with your opponent's coaches.
- When you are called to the center for the decision, thank the referee for calling the bout.
- After the decision, exit as instructed by the referee.
- Cool down slowly after your bout.
- Check with your coach after your bout, and before you leave for the night.

Amateur rules change. Consult a coach or official for up-to-date information.

What to Expect If You Fight on Professional Boxing Cards

As mentioned elsewhere in this book, professional fighting is very different from amateur boxing. Keep in mind that professional cards vary, from small shows at bars to fancy multi-million-dollar cards. The information below is designed to prepare you for what to expect if you participate in a professional boxing event.

Checklist of Items You Need to Pack for Your Fight*
- Your driver's license (or another picture ID)
- Your professional license to fight (issued by the state commissioner), if previously obtained
- Trunks, shoes, socks, tank top/sports bra (females only)
- Copy of your contract

Checklist of Items Your Trainer Will Pack for the Fight*
- Money for fighter's license (if not paid by your manager or promoter)
- Properly-fitted mouthpiece, groin, and/or breast protector
- Gauze and athletic tape for wrapping hands
- Two small towels
- Water bottle
- Tricks of the trade (cotton swabs, grease, enswell, smelling salts, material to treat cuts, butterfly strips, ice bag, etc.)

Press Conference/Interviews

Most professional boxers are expected to help promote the show by giving interviews to journalists (print or television) and possibly by attending a press conference. You will be expected to speak favorably about the promoter and the fight card. Your manager will give you specific instructions about tone and content of your remarks.

Standard Procedures

All boxers will be weighed by the card administrator and checked by a physician. Some states, such as New York, require medical tests (like an EKG), which will be arranged by your manager and/or trainer. Some weigh-ins may take place at the press conference.

Unless you are one of the stars of the card, it is uncommon for you to have your own dressing room, and you may be segregated by sex.

Relationships vary and responsibilities should be established in advance of the fight.

Keys to Successful Competition

The pay for your performance will be set before you agree to the contract (this includes bout pay and/or expenses). Generally, you will be paid after all bouts are over, and usually by check.

You will box four rounds of two minutes (for most women) or three minutes (for men) if you are a beginner. After a few fights at four rounds, you will move up to six rounds, then eight rounds, then ten rounds, and twelve rounds. The size of your gloves (between six and ten ounces) depends on your weight class and the rules of the commission governing your fight. Some promoters choose brands of gloves made of tough leather to promote cuts and bruises. The size of the ring will be negotiated by the promoter and the participants of the main event.

Chapter Six
Social Aspects of Boxing

The Difference Between Professional and Amateur Boxing

Amateur boxing and professional fighting have many differences. Some are subtle while others are obvious to even casual observers. The primary differences lie in philosophy and rules/regulations.

On Philosophy

Amateur boxing is an international Olympic sport, which has undergone a number of rule changes through the years—all in an effort to protect practitioners and raise the standards and quality of boxing. Amateur boxing events are tailored to help protect the health of the boxers. Terms like *boxer* and *bout* are used to signify that amateur boxing is a sport, not a fight. Amateur boxing is characterized by volunteerism and programs designed to give youth and adults an opportunity to participate in a challenging.

In contrast, professional boxing is a business. Professional fighters are paid for their fights. Professional fight cards are organized by promoters, who work with professional managers to make matches between fighters. Federations govern professional boxing and oversee title fights.

In a nutshell, professionals fight and amateurs box. This may seem like an oversimplification of the philosophies of the two, but it clarifies the fundamental differences between them.

On Rules and Regulations

Professional fighting is regulated by state commissions and/or boxing federations, and the rules governing professional fighting vary slightly from commission to commission. Amateur boxing standards are created by the International Amateur Boxing Association (AIBA), the commission for all amateur boxing around the world. Each country has its own national governing body (USA Boxing, Inc., in the United States) which may alter the international rules slightly. All amateur boxing, whether at the Olympics or at a local show, is subject to these rules and its standards must be met by boxers, and certified coaches and officials.

Professionals fight four, six, eight, ten, or twelve rounds of two (for most women) or three (for men) minutes in length. Amateurs box for three or four two-minute rounds. Amateur boxing organizations shortened the round length from three to two minutes after research confirmed that most injuries occurred in the last minute of three-minute rounds.

The role of the referee in amateur boxing is to protect the boxers. In professional fighting, referees often allow fights to continue even after a mismatch occurs. Professional judges score blows based on their effectiveness, but amateur judges score on the *quality and quantity* of blows. A punch which leads to a knockdown in an amateur bout is scored only if it was clean and thrown properly, but a knockdown in a professional fight is likened to a home run in baseball. Amateur referees are empowered to stop any bout in which a serious injury occurs, including the spilling of blood. Professional referees typically allow a boxer's corner to make decisions about injuries, unless they involve the ringside physician to check a severe cut.

Professional matches use two or three judges at ringside, and sometimes the referee serves as the third person to judge fights on a 10-point must system. Professional judges can vote for a draw. Amateur boxing uses three or five certified judges who have the power to take away points for fouls the referee doesn't call. Most amateur bouts are scored via computer.

On Safety

The amateur boxer wears a shirt to protect against getting scraped by the ropes and/or gloves, to keep sweat manageable, and help keep the gloves free of debris and to identify the boxers. The amateur is required to wear a groin protector and headgear that meets specific product safety standards. Physicians are required to sit at ringside at all amateur contests so they can monitor the health of the boxers, as well as check them after their bout is over. Physicians have the power to stop a bout if they see that a boxer is injured. Referees protect boxers by administering a standing-eight count to boxers who appear to be hurt. The gloves that amateurs use are thumbless or thumb-attached, and have significant padding over the knuckles. In the United States, gloves weigh 10 or 12 ounces depending on the boxers' weight. Only 10-ounce gloves are used in international bouts. Some gloves mark the knuckles in white. There are a number of rules regarding fair boxing, and the infraction of a rule is called a foul. In amateur boxing, committing a foul can result in a decrease in the boxer's score, or may even disqualify that boxer if he/she continues to break the rules. Holding is one foul that is monitored closely in amateur boxing. Though infighting is allowed, holding and wrestling are not, since they are dangerous for both boxers. Further, mismatches in amateur boxing

Social Aspects of Boxing

Table 6.1
Differences Between Amateur (Olympic) and Professional Boxing

Aspect	Amateur	Professional	Rationale/Safety
Rules	Are geared to protect the health and safety of the athlete. Uniform in all 190 AIBA-affiliate countries.	Rules vary from country to country, sometimes even within one country.	Uniform rules mean uniform safety standards.
Rounds	4 rounds (3 rounds for females) of 2 minutes each. Shorter rounds for novices and boxers under 17 years of age.	From 4 rounds of 3 minutes up 12 rounds of 3 minutes each. Two-minute rounds for [most] female fights.	Longer bouts are said to increase the risk of injury. For that reason, professional boxing no longer has 15 round fights.
Gloves	10 oz. for [international] competitions. Specially design to cushion the impact. White knuckle-area on glove denotes striking surface. Must have AIBA approved label [for international competition].	6, 8, and 10 ounce gloves, depending on the jurisdiciton.	Not only the weight, but also the design and mater of gloves are factors.
Headguards	Compulsory for all competitions since 1971 in Canada, since 1984 world-wide.	Prohibited.	Headguards reduce cuts by 90%, ear lobe injury by 100%.
Singlets (tops)	Mandatory for all male and female boxers.	Prohibited for males.	Tops prevent rope burns and keep gloves cleaner.
Vaseline, Grease	Prohibited.	Allowed.	Possible eye/vision irritant. Said to prevent "leather burn."
Standing Eight-Count	Given to a boxer having difficulty protecting him/herself. After 3 eight-counts in a round or 4 in total, the bout is stopped.	Usually does not exist.	Purpose is to protect the boxer before he/she gets hurt.
Duties of Referee	First priority is to protect the boxers, and to enforce the rules in the ring. The referee does not keep score.	To enforce the prevailing rules. In some jurisdicitons, the referee keeps score.	The role and actions of the referee are important in preventing serious injuries.
Injuries	The bout is stopped when there is much bleeding, cuts, or swelling around the eye.	The bout is not stopped unless the injured boxer is unable to continue (TKO).	Blood and swelling around the eyes impair vision and make it difficult to defend against blows.
RSC - Outclassed	If a boxer is overmatched, and difficulty defending against a far superior opponent, the referee stops the contest.	No such rule.	Mismatches can lead to injuries, and while rare, can happen in both sports, in spite of rules and all effort to prevent or end them.
Novice Class	Boxers who have competed in events or less are in the Novice Class, and can compete only against other Novices boxers.	No such rule.	The rule seeks to prevent mismatches and to make bouts more even and fair.
Fouls	There are 21 fouls (forbidden, unfair or dangerous tactics) which lead to warnings and point deductions if committed. Disqualificaiton after 3 warnings.	Some tactics considered fouls in amateur boxing are permitted in professional boxing.	Clean boxing without fouls makes the sport safer.
Objectives	To win on points by landing more correct scoring blows on the opponent's target area. knock downs do not result in extra points. Knock-outs are accidental, and not an objective.	For point decisions, agressiveness, knock-downs, injuring ("marking") the opponent also count. Knock-outs are an objective, as a high KO record can lead to higher earnings.	Acute knock-outs are concussions. Less than 1% of amateur bouts end in knock-outs. Over 25% of pro fights end in KOs, ove 50% in KOs and TKOs.
Terms	Coach, Boxer, Bout, Boxing	Trainer, Fighter, Fight, Fighting	

*This chart was provided by the Canadian Amateur Boxing Association. Please note that information in this chart is subject to change as rules change. For more information about Olympic-style boxing, or how to become involved in the Canadian program, visit their website at www.boxing.ca.
1. 12-ounce gloves are used by some national governing bodies (such as the USA).
2. Protect the hands, but make it much easier to knock out opponents. No striking surface marked. Hard leather shells often used to promote cuts. Locally approved.
3. Weight, placement of padding, and material used greatly affect the safety of gloves.
4. Gloves that come in contact with grease can easily pick up debris and transfer it to the opponent's eye.
5. Women's bouts terminate after 2 standing eight-counts in a round and 3 in a bout.

Table 6.2
Additional Differences between Olympic and Professional Boxing

Aspect	Amateur	Professional	Rationale/Safety
Coaching	Usually volunteers, or paid by community organizations. Some coaches are paid directly by their boxers.	Paid by the boxer, manager, and/or promoter.	The role and actions of the support personnel can maximize a boxer's readiness and minimize mismatches.
Judges	3 or 5 at ringside. Certified by national governing body and/or AIBA. AIBA judges may not participate in professional boxing.	2 (if referee is used) or 3 at ringside. May or may not have certification. Professional judges are paid by the show's promoter.	An odd number of judges sitting at ringside can devote full attention to the bout.
Scoring	20-point must (paper scoring) or computer scoring. Points are accumulated only if scoring blow criteria is met.	10-point must system. Points awarded based on hard punches landed in target zone, knockdowns, and knock-outs.	Reflects different objectives of the two sports.
Mercy Rule	In computerized scoring, the jury may stop a bout if one boxer is ahead of the other boxer by more than 15 points.	Does not exist.	Mismatches can lead to injury.
Pay	Olympic-style boxing is considered an amateur sport. Boxers may be allowed reimbursement for expenses. International boxers may receive cash awards for participation from their national governing body.	Boxing is viewed as entertainment. Boxers are paid various amounts, depending on "marketability," as determined by a manager and/or promoter.	Reflect different objectives of the two sports.
Handwraps	Amateur boxers are permitted to use gauze or Velpeau in competition. A small strip of tape is used across the wrist to keep the handwrap from unravelling.	Gauze and tape "casts" are created with large amounts of gauze and tape. Tape may cover the entire hand and wrist with the exception of the knuckles.	Greater amount of wrap and tape allows the boxer to hit harder.
Participation	Open to anyone. Must be under 35 years of age to compete on the Olympic level. Amateur boxers may not participate in professional contests.	Open to anyone viewed as marketable by a manager or promoter.	Reflects different objectives of the two sports: amateur sport versus entertainment industry.

are strictly prohibited, and in the case of an accidental mismatch, the bout can be stopped by the referee. Amateur boxers limit the use of grease (like Vaseline) on their face, since it could interfere with their vision or make gloves sticky and prone to pick up debris that could eventually come into contact with their eyes.

For professionals, holding and other fouls are often allowed. Professionals use smaller gloves made of tougher leather and weighing either six, eight, or ten ounces. Professional gloves are more prone to cause damage like cuts, bruises, and welts because the padding is usually weighted more along the wrist of the glove rather than the knuckles. Professionals are not allowed to wear headgear. The standing-eight count is not in effect in many professional federations, and most fights are allowed to continue until someone is knocked out or injured. Professional male fighters may not wear any kind of shirt, while female pros are encouraged to wear only a sports bra. Grease placed on the face, ears, and body is regularly used by boxers in professional fights to decrease the effectiveness of the opponent's punches.

On Status

Amateur boxing is intense: the action is non-stop and the athletes are generally in excellent physical condition. Amateurs may not box for pay, but they might have opportunities to travel nationally and internationally. Elite boxers who compete internationally often receive some form of reimbursement from their national governing body.

Professional fighters are paid anywhere from $25 per round to millions of dollars per fight. Professionals sometimes receive endorsement opportunities. Professionals, especially heavyweights, may garner popularity. The action is generally slower than amateur boxing, largely because of the greater number of rounds that professionals endure.

The professional promoter's intent to make money is illustrated well in the weight classes of professional events. Professional boxing has numerous weight classes, some of which are only three pounds apart. More classes permit promoters to crown more champions, and thus increase the ticket prices for events that showcase title fights. The high number of professional sanctioning commissions also make more titles available. Lesser-known commissions, thrown together for the sole benefit of promoters' ability to crown more champions, are often called "alphabet soup" commissions.

On Participants

Amateur boxers develop self respect, a sense of pride, respect for others, and they get to participate in a challenging sport. Amateur boxers often develop close relationships with their coaches and often get to be part of a team. Coaches and officials work to keep the boxers' best interest in mind regarding bouts and training regimens.

Trainers, managers, and promoters receive part of the professional boxer's pay (called a purse). Some professional boxers have little say in the fights in which they are matched.

A Short History of Boxing

The exact origins of boxing are not known; however, Egyptian hieroglyphics suggest hand-to-hand combat was practiced as early as 4000 B.C. Most scholars believe boxing was probably practiced and developed by the Greeks, and boxing became an Olympic sport in the 23rd Olympiad in 688 B.C.

Boxing thrived during the Roman era. Fighters may have used

leather bands around their fists to protect their hands as they fought, sometimes to the death. Modern prizefighting emerged in England in the 17th century, and became so popular it was later named England's national sport. A "ring" of spectators contained the fighters, most of whom used dirty tactics such as scratching and gouging, as they fought bare-knuckled for 100 or more rounds. In 1743 Jack Broughton, the second heavyweight champion of England, developed a new set of rules, called the "London Prize Rules," that made some punches illegal and used ropes to make a square "ring."

In the late 1800s, as the sport made its way to the United States, sparring for self-defense gained popularity. The "manly art of self-defense," as it was often called, became mainstream and extremely popular as a pastime. The Marquess of Queensberry supported a new set of rules that limited the number of rounds for participants, made gouging and wrestling illegal, instituted weight classes, judged boxers on a point system, and mandated the use of gloves. With an added emphasis on the science of boxing, amateur programs became recognized around the world.

In 1904, boxing was introduced to the III Modern Olympic Games held in St. Louis. That year, female boxing was an exhibition event. In 1946 the International Amateur Boxing Association (AIBA) was formed, and began to govern Olympic-style amateur boxing for all countries. Additional rules and regulations were designed to protect boxers from unnecessary harm during boxing competitions. Such rules included glove standards, weight standards, mandatory headguards (1984), and electronic scoring (1988).

Though amateur and professional boxing share the spotlight, the "sweet science" is most commonly associated with professional boxing. Approximately 2,500 professional boxers, and 25,000 amateur boxers, are registered annually in the United States alone.

Race and Boxing

The most prevalent social issue surrounding the industry of professional boxing is racism. The bulk of social science research on professional boxing has focused on the plight of Black boxers, illuminating how these prizefighters often find themselves in exploitative relationships with their trainers, managers, and promoters.

History of Race and Boxing

In 1952, Weinberg and Arond conducted the first sociological study of boxers in the U.S. They discovered that professional boxers are usually young urban men or adolescents from lower socioeconomic backgrounds who often share a history of street fighting, an attraction to the money and prestige associated with professional boxing life, or an awareness of or connection to a boxer in their community or family. In addition, researchers found that the boxing subculture exhibits high degrees of stratification between boxers, trainers, managers, and promoters. Trainers polish boxers' skills. Managers, who schedule fights with promoters, directly control boxers' careers and are often perceived by boxers as being interested in "the money first and the man second" (Weinberg & Arond 1952, 466). Consistent with this perception, Weinberg and Arond found that the majority of managers regard boxing as a business and the fighter as a commodity, and are concerned mainly with making money.

Managers negotiate the relationship between the boxer and the promoter, and their dependence upon both often leads managers to secure their relationship with the boxers by making them dependent (i.e., loaning them money). Managers are essential to boxers because they schedule the paying matches, but they often exploit the boxer by overbooking a fighter, overmatching the boxer with superior fighters, forcing the boxer to fight when not in prime condition, and sometimes encouraging the practice of "fixed" fights in which a boxer is instructed to lose intentionally.

While a boxer's manager may have the greatest direct impact on a prizefighter, promoters enjoy the highest level of the hierarchy, concerned foremost with the "show." For instance, promoters are most interested in boxers that are "crowd pleasers," since these fighters draw the biggest following. Often promoters demand a percentage of a manager's "cut" of a good fighter. The relationship between manager and promoter often determines a boxer's career. Weinberg and Arond (1952) explained that boxers are vulnerable to several factors affecting their careers which include structural constraints of upward mobility (based on promoter's business deals), as well as interactions with promoters, managers, and especially trainers who may be driven by their own profit motives.

In his study of Black boxers in Chicago, Hare (1971) found that boxing proved to be positive for some men—"allowing them to escape the deprivation of the slums, but for most, it merely reflects and aggravates their basic oppression" (8). Similarly, Sugden (1987) argues that the "exploitation of disadvantage" leads to the practice of intentionally locating the ghetto boxing gym in the center of urban poverty so managers can recruit raw street-fighting talent. Loic Wacquant's "sociology of pugilism" describes the boxing gym as a place nurtured and held together "by definite social forces and cultural repertoires [and that it] arises and reproduces itself both as reflections of and reaction against street culture" (1992, 225).

It is no coincidence that professional gyms are often located in poor areas of major cities, where managers and promoters recruit poor men (and women) trying to escape their poverty by entering into professional contracts.

The Great White Hope

Boxing demographics traditionally mirror the changes in ethnic composition among members of urban lower strata—at the turn of the century the Irish dominated boxing, by 1928 Jewish boxers had succeeded them, by 1936 Italian boxers moved to the forefront, and, since 1948, Blacks have dominated the sport (Hare, 1971; Sugden, 1987; Wacquant, 1992; Weinberg & Arond, 1952). In 1971, Blacks comprised more than 70% of all boxers (Hare, 1971). Some suggest that along with changes in urban demographics Latinos are now challenging Blacks for domination of the sport (Sugden, 1987). This ethnic tradition, coupled with prevalent racism, provides a foundation for the "great white hope" phenomenon to thrive in the United States (Hare, 1971).

When boxing promoters realized that racist fans (in the United States and elsewhere) were interested in seeing white champions, the hope for a great white boxer emerged. Promoters often pitted white champions against Black opponents in order to fuel racist attitudes and further build audience interest in seeing white men as victors.

Racism still exists in professional boxing. However, many people argue that the situation for non-white boxers has improved. In some regards this may be true: Mike Tyson and Evander Holyfield are top-paid boxers. Oscar De La Hoya is a star. However, examples of successful minorities cannot replace the reality of the most common experience: that most Black and Latino boxers are generally underpaid, underappreciated, and undermarketed compared to white boxers.

Racism and Classism

In the United States, race and class tend to go together, since racial minorities are over-represented on the lower end of the economic spectrum. The exploitative relationships between Black or Latino boxers and their managers/promoters also exist between white boxers and their handlers. Overall, the boxer, no matter what his/her race, is controlled by an elite group of promoters and managers who make money off of the prizefighter.

Managers will typically require that prizefighters sign contracts that include a percentage "cut" of the boxer's gross pay. The standard cut is 33 percent, but is sometimes negotiated as a smaller percentage. Contracts will also specify the number of fights per year expected of a fighter, and will include a no-compete statement which bars the fighter from fighting on a card not organized by the manager. Most contracts specify a time commitment of three to five years, often giving the right of renewal exclusively to the manager, giving a boxer little recourse if he/she is unhappy with the management. Finally, managers and promoters work together to organize shows, so managers often work with a select number of promoters. Therefore, with the exception of a few boxers who actually make it to the "big time," boxers will stay in the same network of managers and promoters throughout their careers.

Tolerance Among Boxers

Though professional boxing is often characterized by exploitative relationships, the boxers themselves seem to have a fundamental respect for each other. This is especially evident on the amateur level in which boxers often share the gym with teammates from diverse backgrounds. When speaking of racism in boxing, it is often the managers, promoters, and crowds that display racist attitudes, not the boxers themselves.

Finding Out More About Race in the Sport of Boxing

Many books and articles address race in professional boxing:

Hare, N. (1971). "A study of the black fighter." *The Black Scholar* November: 2-8.

Sugden, J. (1987). "The exploitation of disadvantage: The occupational sub-culture of the boxer." *The Sociological Review Monograph* 33: 187-209.

Wacquant, L. (1992). "The social logic of boxing in black Chicago: Toward a sociology of pugilism." *Sociology of Sport Journal* 9: 221-54.

Weinberg, S. K. and H. Arond (1952). "The occupational culture of the boxer." *American Journal of Sociology* 52: 460-69

A number of movies depict elements of racism and/or classism in boxing, such as: *Raging Bull, On the Waterfront, The Great White Hype, The Hurricane, Don King: Only in America, The Great White Hope.*

Women in Boxing

The most provocative and hotly discussed topic by people both inside and outside of amateur and professional boxing is the issue of gender inclusiveness. What follows is the history of women's involvement in the sport, as well as some of the issues that affect female boxers who participate in the *sweet science*.

History of Women's Involvement in Professional Boxing

Women appeared as prizefighters in the early 1700s, in England. The first advertised women's prizefight in the United States took place in 1888, in New York, between Alice Leary and Hattie Leslie (*Boxing Illustrated* 1974). The majority of the women boxers in the 1880s and early 1900s performed in carnival shows, theaters, and saloons. Unlike their male counterparts, women boxer's popularity was tied to their value as a gendered spectacle. In the 1940s and 50s, women like "Battling" Barbara Buttrick began to make headlines as they stepped into the ring in an attempt to prove women could box on a more serious level.

In the mid-1970s and early 1980s women's professional boxing began to increase in popularity and receive popular media coverage. Women like Marian "Tyger" Trimiar, Jackie Tonawanda, and Cathy "Cat" Davis challenged their state commissions for official professional boxing licenses. Women's boxing became organized through the Women's Boxing Board (WBB), dedicated to "the cause of women's boxing." In spite of the growing popularity of women's prizefighting, the WBB collapsed in the mid-80s. However, women's boxing once again began to become popular in the 1990s, largely to the credit of three major factors: boxercise, executive boxing, and other fitness-boxing programs; the advent of women's opportunities in the amateur ranks; and the move of Don King to actively promote a woman boxer, Christy Martin, whose slugger-style won the hearts of many boxing aficionados when she appeared on the Tyson-Seldon pay-per-view undercard. Many fans soon clamored to see more women's boxing.

Currently, about 800 women register as professional fighters each year in the United States. Most professional bouts take place in Nevada, Florida, and New York. On August 3, 1993 a woman's match debuted on national cable television, when a portion of a Jr. Welterweight bout between Helga Risoy and Delia Gonzales aired on USA Network's *Tuesday Night Fights*. Since then, more women's bouts have been covered on broadcast and cable television, as well as on Pay-Per-View. However, women's boxing is still not covered extensively by television nor by boxing magazines.

As women's professional boxing began to grow, so did an opportunity to organize and promote it. In the early 1990s, Barbra Buttrick spearheaded an attempt to organize the women's sport through her Women's International Boxing Federation (WIBF). A couple of years later came the International Female Boxing Association (IFBA), led by promotion company Event Entertainment, and the International Women's Boxing Federation (IWBF) organized by Freddie Guooberwhich in New York. These three organizations and other commissions now compete to sanction women's professional fights and championships. As a result of this, and typical promoter disputes, many of the women boxers considered to be the best have difficulty finding opportunities to fight each other, and thus miss out on potentially large paydays.

History of Women's Involvement in Amateur Boxing

Until October 1993, women were not permitted to join the United States Amateur Boxing Association (USA Boxing, Inc.)—the association that is responsible for regulating all amateur boxing in the United States and which serves as male boxers' stepping-stone into the Olympic Games. Two women have sued USA Boxing for the right to compete. In the early 1980s, Gail Grandchamp filed a lawsuit in Massachusetts in an effort to achieve amateur standing. Though she turned professional before the court's ruling affected her status because the lawsuit took more than ten years, Massachusetts lost the case and, for a while, was the only state that allowed women to register as amateurs.

In March of 1993, Dallas Malloy of Washington filed a federal lawsuit with the American Civil Liberties Union challenging USA Boxing's discriminatory policies. USA Boxing, Inc. eventually agreed to develop a national women's amateur division. The United States joined other countries including Canada, Finland, and Sweden in allowing women the chance to box as amateurs. Every year more countries join the movement. USAB now registers more than 2,000 women and girls each year, many of whom hope that women's boxing will one day be an Olympic sport. This dream could become a reality as early as 2008 as more and more countries support women's Olympic-style boxing.

Sexism in the sport

As women gain the right to compete, and fight for legitimacy in amateur and professional boxing, they are often met with discrimination. Some people in boxing do not want to see women succeed, or they try to take advantage of women who want to box. Some coaches do not allow women to train in their gyms. Others don't pay attention to women who attempt to train there. Still, women have persevered and worked to compete in the sport.

Professional women boxers are often marketed as sex symbols, rather than as pugilists. Fight posters that read "Leather and Lace" and "Lips of Rouge: Fists of Fury" are reminders of women's social location in the sport. In order to maximize their marketability, some female prizefighters even dress provocatively both inside and outside the ring.

Like male fighters, women pugilists often have exploitative relationships with their trainers, managers, and promoters. However, the issue of pay reveals an interesting trend in the women's side of the boxing industry. Male pugilists often make very little money before they become established professionals. However, once a male boxer becomes well known he may begin to make large sums of money. Championship bouts may bring a male boxer a purse of more than one million dollars (the most well-known prizefighters make several million for one fight). On the other side, some women boxers may be able to hold out for $200 to $2,000 for their first fights. However, with a typical workload of two to five bouts per year, most women pugilists are not able to make ends meet on a prizefighter's salary. Additionally, the most money paid to a woman boxer for a championship bout is currently $5,000. When Christy Martin announced a contract with Don King for $100,000 per fight, she became the highest-paid woman boxer in history.

Most recently, women's professional boxing has been marked by the promotion of the "famous daughters" of Muhammed Ali, Joe Frazier, George Foreman, and others. Laila Ali, Jacqui Frazier, and Freeda Foreman demanded high pay at their introduction to the sport, marketing their names, rather than their boxing skills. None of these boxers developed as amateurs, yet they currently make more money per bout than professionals who rise through the ranks.

Supporting Women Boxers

Women's entry into boxing has brought a new excitement to the sport, both on the amateur and professional levels. Women's professional bouts are often more active than their male counterparts, due in part to many sanctioning bodies forcing women to fight only two-minute rounds. (Some men's commissions have also considered shortening rounds, but have not yet done so, likely because of tradition.)

In order to be successful, female boxers need the support of other boxers, coaches, and fans. So far, it seems that both amateur and professional boxing benefit from the vitality of female boxers.

Finding Out More About Women's Boxing

Research on women's boxing can be found in the following articles:

Halbert, C. (1997). "Tough Enough and Woman Enough: Stereotypes, Discrimination, and Impression Management Among Women Professional Boxers," *Journal of Sport and Social Issues*, vol. 21, no. 1, pp. 7-36.

Hargreaves, J. (1996). "Bruising Peg to boxerobics: Gendered boxing—images and meanings." in *Boxer: An anthology of writings on boxing and visual culture*. D. Chandler, J. Gill, T. Guha and G. Tawadros. Cambridge, MIT Press: 121-131.

The following websites are dedicated to boxing, and have specific information on female boxing: www.usaboxing.org, www.boxing.ca, www.womenboxing.com, and www.BoxingResource.com. You might also check out the documentary films *On the Ropes* and *Shadow Boxers*.

The Romance of Boxing

Adversity, sweat, blood...victory! This is the winning combination that characterizes the typical boxing story. The hero overcomes adversity by working hard and facing a challenge. In the movies, the grit of boxing is romanticized in the crowning of a good champion over a mean-spirited opponent. These days the use of boxing symbols and terminology seems almost commonplace.

Boxing is currently experiencing a surge in interest. Amateur boxing programs around the world are growing for men and women. College boxing programs are expanding. Women are now competing in amateur and professional boxing like never before. Executive boxing and aerobic boxing programs are promoting a new kind of fitness for people who would never have imagined strapping on a pair of gloves. We see competitive boxers with product endorsements, and models dressed in boxing gear selling underwear. Boxing is everywhere.

In fact, people are infatuated with boxing: just consider the sport's history. Boxing represents the American dream: you can become a wealthy champion if you just work hard enough. There are many stories about down-and-out kids who became world boxing champions, and about street kids who found—through amateur boxing—that there is more for them in life. These are the stories that get press, further fueling the belief that boxing is a "way out" of adverse life conditions.

Ironically, as popular as boxing is, it is not well understood nor respected. Mostly this is due to the professional industry's focus on entertainment rather than sport. Though they are similar in nature, amateur and professional boxing have little in common. There has been some governmental regulation of professional boxing in recent years in an effort to counter the exploitative nature of that industry.

Medicine and Boxing Controversy: Head Trauma

Some medical professionals are calling for a ban on professional boxing, citing the fact that boxers have actually been killed in the ring. Though other sports have experienced similar tragedies, proponents of a ban declare that boxers put themselves in harm's way purposefully. Others, however, argue that the sport of amateur boxing remains safe.

The fact that Olympic-style boxing enforces rules, mandates safety equipment, and encourages a philosophy of boxing—rather than fighting—distinguishes it from the professional sport. However, boxing (whether amateur or professional) can still be a dangerous sport, since the participants are purposefully striking each other. Anyone participating in contact sports must understand that their participation carries a risk of serious injury or death. Though medical professionals disagree on the physical merits of amateur boxing, they do agree amateur boxing is preferable to professional fighting.

Studies have shown amateur boxing ranks low in occurrence of injury and fatality. *The National Youth Sports Safety Foundation* published an article on the prevention of athletic head and spine injuries and didn't mention amateur boxing among the sports that carry risk of such injury (Cantu, 1996). Amateur boxing is statistically safer than sports like automobile racing, horseback riding, football, soccer, swimming, and even gymnastics—all of which lead to many more injuries and deaths per year than amateur boxing.

Although amateur rules were created to protect participants, there are some risks to boxing about which all participants should be educated. Whether amateur or professional, concerns about the impact of punches to the brain are numerous.

The head is vulnerable in boxing since it is a target area. Violent or repeated trauma to the head should be avoided. A boxer who is hurt from a head blow (whether in practice or competition) should not continue the bout. Also, sparring should be done in controlled environments, and only minimally, in comparison to other training techniques such as skill-building, strategy work, and cardiovascular training. Keeping sparring intensity in check, and the frequency low, helps minimize the effect such trauma may have on the brain (Jordan, Matser, Zimmerman, Zazula, 1996).

Amateur boxers who are knocked down (either touching the canvas with a hand or knee, or being out on their feet) as a result of a head blow will receive an RSCH from the referee, which mandates a thorough check by the ringside physician, as well as by the boxer's healthcare provider. A boxer who receives an RSCH has a mandatory waiting period for sparring and competing lasting for at least 30 days.

Recently, all athletes have been made aware of the risk of Second Impact Syndrome (SIS) which is common among football and soccer players. SIS results from repeated trauma to the head, and can be avoided by checking with healthcare providers about boxing, taking time off from sparring if you are hit hard, and limiting time spent sparring and competing. "Punch drunk" prizefighters are believed to have damaged their brains by sparring/fighting in small gloves and without headgear, almost every day of their training. Experts now know sparring should be done in moderation. Additionally, Olympic-style rules limit the number of rounds/minutes a boxer competes in the ring.

To reduce your risk of Second Impact Syndrome, do the following: 1) always be honest with healthcare professionals when they ask about your history of headaches, 2) make note of *any* symptoms or abnormal feelings you might have such as dizziness, blurred vision, confusion, problems with concentration, memory loss, etc., 3) limit the amount of free-form sparring that you do in training, 4) always use well-fitting headgear in competition and training, and use gloves of at least 12 ounces in sparring sessions, 5) sharpen your defensive skills for use in sparring and competition, and 6) strengthen your neck muscles in order to minimize the whiplash effect when hit to the head.

Chapter Seven
Coaching and Training Boxers

The Responsibility of the Coach

Honing a boxer is a difficult and laborious job that requires attention to boxers' mental and physical needs. The boxing coach (or trainer) has the most difficult and important job in boxing. You must prepare the boxer mentally and physically; watch for and correct mistakes in technique; teach rules and regulations; remind the boxer about healthy lifestyle habits; scout his/her opponents; make sure he/she is evenly matched in bouts; and take responsibility for the boxer before, during, and after the bout.

Coaches have to know the training styles of all their boxers, and know how each boxer responds to different coaching strategies. Coaches respond to boxers' needs in and outside the ring. They learn when boxers need words of encouragement to counter the criticisms they hear. Coaches learn when to protect boxers by retiring them before they get hurt in a bout. Between rounds, coaches attend to injury, such as a bloody nose, provide water, and give clear instructions to the boxer. Throughout practices and competition, coaches set the tone for expectations, as boxers look to coaches for cues about how to act.

Among all of the different responsibilities to boxers, the coach has one sole purpose: to help the boxer reach his or her full potential within a safe training and competition environment. Coaching boxers can be a rewarding experience as you watch each boxer develop mentally and physically.

Items typically found in the corner:
- water bucket with sponge
- ice
- water bottle
- towel to wipe boxer
- towel to wipe floor
- stopwatch to time the round
- swab sticks to stop a bleeding nose or to clean a wound
- gauze to wrap hands before bout
- athletic tape to secure hand wraps and laces outside the gloves
- scissors to cut tape
- gauze pads
- latex gloves

First Aid for Minor Injuries

This essay does not replace the services of a medical professional. If your injury causes you great pain, or is persistent, or is more serious in nature, you should visit your healthcare provider to get a full assessment of the injury and learn how best to treat it. However, if you have a minor injury such as a superficial scrape, a minor ankle or wrist sprain, or shin pains, then use this simple self-treatment. Follow the R.I.C.E. guidelines (outlined below) within the first 24 hours of your injury.

> *Rest:* stay off your feet so you don't aggravate the injury while it heals.
> *Ice:* apply ice to the area within 10-15 minutes of the injury. Repeat intermittent icing (or ice massage) for 10-30 minutes at intervals of 30-45 minutes.
> *Compression:* use an elastic bandage to minimize swelling to the area.
> *Elevation:* prop up the affected area (above heart level) while you rest and/or sleep.

The R.I.C.E. method will reduce swelling, which will speed healing and decrease the pain you feel in that area. If your pain is persistent, however, you should consult a healthcare professional.

It is always best to treat an injury so that it does not become a chronic problem. If, for example, you begin to have pain in your shin, then a regimen of added stretching and R.I.C.E. can possibly heal the injury before it develops into a more serious one (like shin splints).

If you are prone to injuring certain muscles, then be sure to increase your warm-up, cool-down, and stretching to reduce the risk of re-injury. If you have a chronic injury, it is best to consult medical personnel who can prescribe anti-inflammatory drugs and/or a rehabilitation program to aid recovery and prevent further injury.

It is best to take some added time to heal a small problem rather than take a lot of time trying to heal a serious injury. Injury prevention, accomplished by warming up/cooling down, stretching, and performing exercises properly, is the best way to be sure that your training goes uninterrupted.

Boxing Truths and Myths

Water will make me heavy in the ring.

False. You would have to drink massive amounts of water in order for the weight to affect you before your bout. However, you do need to be properly hydrated for your bout. If you deprive your body of fluids, you can compreomise your strength, speed, and recovery.

I don't have to be in shape as long as I'm smarter than my opponent.

False. Never underestimate your opponent. If you are not prepared physically for competition, then you risk losing or getting hurt. Even the smartest of boxers can be overwhelmed by a boxer who is both smart and fit.

A good offense is the best defense.

False. Defense is critical. Even the best boxers will get hit sometimes. Without defensive skills you can't protect yourself. In an evenly scored bout, the boxer with the best style (including the ability to evade punches) will be awarded the bout by judges.

Superstitions are stupid.

Not necessarily. Though superstitions are generally believed to be baseless, the mind can be powerful. Individuals may convince themselves that they can increase their luck in order to feel like they have more control of a situation. If you believe that a particular pair of socks will bring you luck, then by all means wear the socks; however, you will have to eventually deal with the fact that the socks will wear out.

Putting steak on my eye will reduce the effects of a black eye.

True, sort of. The cooling action of the steak will help reduce the swelling of your eye as will an ice bag or even a bag of frozen peas.

Drinking milk the day of my bout will make it harder to breathe.

True. Milk and milk-based products, such as cheese and ice cream, often increase production of mucous in the mouth and sinus cavities. This may translate into a feeling of labored breathing. To avoid this feeling, reduce your intake of milk products the day of your bout. Otherwise, make sure you ingest enough calcium-rich foods to ensure a balanced diet.

If I box, I will end up with brain damage.
False. Though the research concerning head trauma is conflicting, most physicians agree that amateur boxing, and moderate sparring with proper equipment, is relatively safe. There are some former prominent professional boxers, like Muhammed Ali, who seem to suffer the effects of a professional career in boxing. Most believe that Ali's Parkinson's disease may have been accelerated by repeatedly being hit in the head, and although there is no evidence of this being true, it seems a logical conclusion. Ali boxed during a time when there were few safety mechanisms in place for boxers, such as headgear and padded gloves. Additionally, Ali was a professional fighter and was quite active in competition and in sparring. See the chapter on medical findings for more information on boxing and head trauma research, and talk to your personal healthcare provider if you have concerns about your own risk.

I need to compete every weekend if I want to be a good boxer.
Good boxers stay active. This means about two matches (or tournaments) a month during the peak season. Balance time for recovery and refining technique with gaining experience at competitions.

I can cut weight before my bout, and then rehydrate right after weigh-ins.
False. Physicians now believe the body needs at least 24 hours to rehydrate after losing significant amounts of fluid. Sauna suits are dangerous. If you lose too much water weight, you compromise your performance, fitness, and health. If you want to lose weight, do so gradually in order to minimize ill effects.

Fouling in a bout gives me an advantage.
False. Fouling is cheating and can also be dangerous, since you are vulnerable while you are attempting to foul.

Sex the night before a bout will leave me tired for my bout.
True and False. Though there is no evidence to suggest that sex depletes a boxer's energy, most boxers find that training for a bout is a good excuse not to spend any emotional or physical energy on relationships or activities that might lead to sex.

Fitness Boxing

In the early 1990s it became fashionable for executives in New York to start working out in boxing gyms. This began a fitness trend called "Executive Boxing." Executive boxing appeals to men and women who work in white-collar jobs, and rarely get to participate in activities as physically exciting and challenging as boxing. Most executive boxers work out with other fitness and competitive boxers and spar with other executives.

Soon after the trend began, executive boxing was modified somewhat into a boxing program that was aerobic in nature. Known by many names, such as boxing aerobics, boxaerobics, and boxercize, this craze hit aerobics and fitness gyms across the U.S. in the mid- to late 1990s. Boxaerobics attracts women and men who desire a challenging and unique fitness workout. Most boxaerobics programs do not include sparring, but rather encourage shadowboxing, air-punching combinations, and defenseive moves that work the total body. Some boxaerobics programs include punching bags and focus mitts, something very few people have ever experienced.

Executive and boxaerobics programs expose a great number of people to the sport of boxing. Those who participate in fitness boxing are able to develop an appreciation for the skills and fitness level required of boxers who train to compete.

It is important to support executive boxers and fitness boxers who may be training in your gym, or at a local club. Lend your support by holding focus mitts or by giving constructive feedback for someone on the fitness level. Let them throw punches at you sometimes while you practice your defensive skills. Fitness boxers will love the challenge, and you will be a model for what boxing does best: bring diverse people together for the love of the sport.

Fitness boxers, too, should be supportive of competitive boxers. It takes a lot of nerve to work out in a boxing gym, but it takes much more to step through the ropes and compete. Show your support by attending matches, by donating supplies to the gym, or helping with fundraisers for amateur programs. Give something back to the coaches and athletes that make boxing so much fun for you.

Chapter Eight
Supportive Material

Supportive Material

Table 8.1
Offensive Arsenal Summary

Type	Technique	Also Known As	Description
Punches	Jab	#1	thrown with the lead hand (the left hand for right-handers) Types: traditional, upper, stiff, and blinding
Punches	Cross	#2; power punch	thrown with the strong hand (the right hand for right-handers) Types: straight, short (quick), and overhand
Punches	Hook	#3	a swing-type punch thrown with the lead hand Types: long, mid, and short (inside)
Punches	Uppercut	#4 (strong hand) or #5 (lead hand)	thrown with the palm facing you, this punch moves straight up the opponent to land on either the head or body Types: long and short
Punches	Counterpunch		a punch thrown after the opponent leads with a punch, with the intention of capitalizing on a miss or hole left in the opponent's defensive stance
Movement	Drawing		a strategic offensive tactic in which you leave an opening purposely, in an attempt to "draw" your opponent into leading with a specific punch that you can then counterpunch
Movement	In-fighting		boxing within very close range of the opponent, often consists of body punches
Movement	Angle	side step	moving to the side of the opponent, so that you are in position to contact the opponent, while simultaneously moving out of range of the opponent's punches
Movement	Angle on approach	v-step on approach	the action of approaching your opponent at an angle, rather than meeting him/her directly
Movement	Feint		an offensive technique in which you pretend to throw a punch in order to provoke an offensive or defensive counter from your opponent.

Table 8.2
Defensive Arsenal Summary

Type	Technique	Also Known As	Description
Hand Counters	Parry	catch	the action of meeting the knuckles of the punch with the open glove so as to catch or deflect it.
Hand Counters	Block	absorb	the deflection of a punch using the back of the gloves, forearms, elbows, arms, or shoulders.
Hand Counters	Guard		a stance in which the gloves, forearms, or shoulders are postioned to defend specific area(s) of the head and/or body.
Hand Counters	Clinch		a tactic used when in-fighting, in which one boxer attempts to lift or hold the opponent's arms in order to prevent him/her from punching. If both boxers are clinched, the referee will command "break." If only one boxer clinches, the referee may call a holding foul.
Hand Counters	Hold		a situation in which one boxer grabs the other's gloves, arms, body, or head. Holding is a foul.
Integrative Maneuvers	Duck		an evasive move in which the legs are bent so the opponent's punches miss overhead.
Integrative Maneuvers	Slip		an evasive move in which the legs and waist are bent over the thigh of the strong-side leg to allow the oncoming punch to move past the ear.
Integrative Maneuvers	Slide	slip to the lead side	an evasive move in which the legs and waist are bent over the thigh of the lead leg to allow the oncoming punch to move past the ear.
Integrative Maneuvers	Roll		moving the head and/or body along the same path as the oncoming punch to prevent it from reaching the target at full impact.
Integrative Maneuvers	U-dip		ducking while simultaneously moving the upper body to the right/left, or forward/backward.
Integrative Maneuvers	Weave		an evasive move in which the legs and torso are bent to move the body down and around punches to avoid being hit (weaving around the punches).
Integrative Maneuvers	Bob		ducking down and up to evade punches.
Directional Maneuvers	Half-step back		movement of the legs and torso in which the back foot moves straight backwards and the front foot remains in place, ready to spring the body forward into the boxing stance or an offensive attack.
Directional Maneuvers	Side step		movement to the side of the opponent, in order to create an angle from which to attack while simultaneously moving out of range of the opponent's punches.
Directional Maneuvers	Backpedal	bicycle	quick retreat backwards while still facing the opponent.

Supportive Material

Table 8.3
Defensive Strategies for Opponent's Punches

Opponent's Punches	Gloves, Elbows, Shoulders					Torso							Legs				
	Block/Absorb			Parry		Slip/Slide			Duck/U-dip			Roll	Moving/Taking Angles				
	w/ the glove	w/ the shoulder	w/ the forearm/elbow	w/ the glove	w/ the forearm/elbow	to their strong side	to their weak side	half-step back	straight down	downward and to their strong side	downward and to their weak side	in the direction of the punch	backward to their strong side	backward to their weak side	straight back	forward towards their strong side	forward towards their weak side
Straight jab to the head	✓	.	✓	✓	.	✓	✓	✓	✓	.	✓	✓	✓	✓	✓	✓	.
Straight jab to the body	.	✓	.	.	✓	.	.	✓	.	.	.	.	✓	✓	✓	✓	.
Straight cross to the head	✓	.	✓	✓	.	✓	✓	✓	✓	.	✓	✓	✓	✓	✓	.	✓
Straight cross to the body	.	✓	.	.	✓	.	.	✓	.	.	.	.	✓	✓	✓	.	✓
Lead hook to the head	✓	.	✓	.	.	.	✓	✓	.	.	.	✓	✓	.	✓	✓	.
Lead hook to the body	.	.	.	.	✓	✓	.	✓	✓	✓	.	✓	✓	.	✓	✓	.
Strong hook to the head	✓	.	✓	.	.	✓	.	✓	.	.	.	✓	.	.	✓	.	✓
Strong hook to the body	.	.	.	.	✓	.	✓	✓	✓	✓	.	✓	.	.	✓	.	✓
Lead uppercut to the head	✓	.	✓	.	.	.	✓	✓	.	✓	.	.	✓	.	✓	✓	.
Lead uppercut to the body	.	.	.	.	✓	.	.	✓	.	.	.	.	✓	.	✓	✓	.
Strong uppercut to the head	✓	.	✓	.	.	✓	.	✓	.	.	.	.	.	.	✓	.	✓
Strong uppercut to the body	.	.	.	.	✓	.	✓	✓	.	.	.	.	.	.	✓	.	✓

What Are Your Goals for Boxing?

Short-term goals:

_____
_____
_____
_____
_____
_____

Mid-range goals:

_____
_____
_____
_____
_____
_____
_____

Long-term goals:

_____
_____
_____
_____
_____
_____

Supportive Material

Combinations Worksheet

A combination is a set of punches that flow together with the intention of scoring against your opponent. Some combinations consist of only two punches, others might involve as many as six or seven punches. Practicing combinations will help you throw multiple punches while engaged in competition. There are many other combinations to learn and practice.

You can create your own combinations by keeping the following guidelines in mind:

- Throw upstairs and downstairs, up the middle and on the outside, of your opponent.
- Incorporate defensive moves (such as ducking and taking angles).
- Practice slowly to make sure the combination flows smoothly.

Use this worksheet to catalog combinations you learn in the gym, or combinations you create yourself.

Combination 1: _____
_____
_____
_____

Combination 2: _____
_____
_____
_____

Combination 3: _____
_____
_____
_____

Combination 4: _____
_____
_____
_____

Combination 5: _____
_____
_____
_____

Combination 6: _____
_____
_____
_____

Combination 7: _____
_____
_____
_____

Combination 8: _____
_____
_____
_____

Combination 9: _____
_____
_____
_____

Combination 10: _____
_____
_____
_____

Supportive Material

Self-Assessment of Mastery of Boxing Skills

Boxing requires the perfect coordination of a number of skills. Becoming a complete boxer is a process. While your coach guides your development in every facet of training, monitor your progress and know with which skills you feel most comfortable.

Use the skills list below to rate yourself on each of the following areas needed to be an ultimate (and successful) boxer. Make an honest assessment of your current level of mastery (needs work, average, good, or mastered) to discover your own strengths and weaknesses.

Offense/Defense

	Not Yet Learned	Needs Work	Average	Good	Mastered
1. Confidence in jab	❏	❏	❏	❏	❏
2. Confidence in power hand	❏	❏	❏	❏	❏
3. Confidence in hook	❏	❏	❏	❏	❏
4. Confidence in uppercuts	❏	❏	❏	❏	❏
5. Ability to punch with speed (both hands)	❏	❏	❏	❏	❏
6. Ability to punch with strength (both hands)	❏	❏	❏	❏	❏
7. Ability to punch with power (speed + strength) with either hand	❏	❏	❏	❏	❏
8. Giving the lead shoulder when in the boxing zone	❏	❏	❏	❏	❏
9. Ability to punch at will	❏	❏	❏	❏	❏
10. Moving to the left	❏	❏	❏	❏	❏
11. Moving to the right	❏	❏	❏	❏	❏
12. Ability to punch off-balance	❏	❏	❏	❏	❏
13. Ability to punch while moving	❏	❏	❏	❏	❏
14. Taking angles, not merely moving forward or backward while boxing	❏	❏	❏	❏	❏
15. Responding to opponent's style instantly	❏	❏	❏	❏	❏
16. Acting, not reacting—thinking ahead	❏	❏	❏	❏	❏
17. Ability to control opponent with the jab	❏	❏	❏	❏	❏
18. Seeing openings and hitting them	❏	❏	❏	❏	❏
19. Using the entire ring during any round	❏	❏	❏	❏	❏
20. Ability to stay active during each round for the entire bout	❏	❏	❏	❏	❏
21. Catching opponent's jab	❏	❏	❏	❏	❏
22. Slipping and sliding punches to the head	❏	❏	❏	❏	❏
23. Ducking opponent's punches	❏	❏	❏	❏	❏
24. Turning defense into offense	❏	❏	❏	❏	❏
25. Accurate placement of punches	❏	❏	❏	❏	❏

Style and Adaptability in Bouts

	Not Yet Learned	Needs Work	Average	Good	Mastered
26. Ability to feint	☐	☐	☐	☐	☐
27. Ability to draw	☐	☐	☐	☐	☐
28. Infighting	☐	☐	☐	☐	☐
29. Ability to vary punches with speed and intensity	☐	☐	☐	☐	☐
30. Shots are difficult for opponent to read	☐	☐	☐	☐	☐
31. Boxing backwards	☐	☐	☐	☐	☐
32. Ability to get away from opponent when necessary	☐	☐	☐	☐	☐
33. Staying out of corners on defense	☐	☐	☐	☐	☐
34. Staying focused through entire bout	☐	☐	☐	☐	☐
35. Hearing referee's commands to stop/break	☐	☐	☐	☐	☐
36. Ability to engage quickly after referee's command to box	☐	☐	☐	☐	☐
37. Ability to box for judges	☐	☐	☐	☐	☐
38. Ability to follow directions of coach	☐	☐	☐	☐	☐
39. Ability to change strategies in the middle of the bout, when instructed by coach	☐	☐	☐	☐	☐
40. Feeling in control during the bout	☐	☐	☐	☐	☐
41. Feeling confident before/during the bout	☐	☐	☐	☐	☐

Practicing Techniques

	Not Yet Learned	Needs Work	Average	Good	Mastered
42. Positive attitude toward boxing practice	☐	☐	☐	☐	☐
43. Ability to work new skills when sparring	☐	☐	☐	☐	☐
44. Staying focused during practices	☐	☐	☐	☐	☐
45. Running or completing other cardiovascular workouts at least 4 times per week	☐	☐	☐	☐	☐
46. Ability to teach boxing stance and basic punches to new boxers	☐	☐	☐	☐	☐

Notes about training or competition:

_____
_____
_____
_____
_____
_____
_____

Supportive Material

Getting Involved in the Sport

Finding a Gym

Boxing gyms are generally divided into two types of clubs: fitness gyms and traditional boxing gyms. Variations of each are typically found in metropolitan areas.

Many fitness gyms have incorporated boxing equipment in their aerobics classes. However, fitness classes are typically not taught by people educated in the skills of boxing. If you are interested in learning techniques used in actual competition, you should visit a boxing gym.

Traditional boxing gyms are staffed by coaches (volunteer or paid) experienced in competitive boxing. These gyms contain boxing equipment, where competition techniques are practiced. Boxing gyms may lack fitness equipment.

Traditional boxing gyms may range from four to 100 members; they may or may not charge a fee to join; membership may be limited to competitive boxers: professionals only, amateurs only, or both. They may receive public funding and thus play a specific role in their community. It is important to ask whether the gym carries insurance for those using the facility; ask whether the gym is registered with the national governing body. Also, before you join, be sure to determine the cost of personal training.

Boxing workouts may be open workouts (allowing you to work at your own pace with a coach) or collective workouts (where boxers attend scheduled classes). Boxing gyms and boxing coaches have wildly varying styles, so shop around for a gym that meets your needs.

Whether you choose a fitness or a boxing gym will depend on your training goals. If you choose to work out at a boxing gym, be sure to tell the coaches which style of training you desire—amateur or professional. Explain your particular fitness goals and let coaches know whether you want to spar or compete. The style of boxing you choose will greatly influence the type of workout and the techniques you will learn.

Three ways to find a traditional boxing gym include: Attending local shows and asking organizers about gyms in your area; looking in the phone book under boxing gyms, martial arts, or gymnasiums; and calling or visiting the website of the national governing body in your country for contact information of registered amateur gyms in your area.

Volunteer Opportunities

There are many ways for volunteers to support amateur boxing. There is always a need for fundraisers, ticket-takers, concession stand workers, clerks, timekeepers, judges, referees, boxing show producers, ringside physicians, dentists to make fitted mouthpieces, video camera operators, individuals to help set up and repair the ring, or even uniform designs. You may want to consider trading some of your services for membership to the gym.

Finding Competition

Every country that wishes to compete internationally in amateur boxing must have a national organizing body. Information on organizing bodies can be obtained through the Olympic office in your country.

Professional commissions organize and govern professional boxing championships in every country. Local professional shows are managed by state commissions, along with promoters and managers. For information on finding local professional shows and/or opportunities to box, visit your local boxing gym. All boxing gyms will have contact information for amateur and professional opportunities.

Informational Websites

International Amateur Boxing Association *www.aiba.net*

European Amateur Boxing Association *www.eaba.org*

United States Amateur Boxing Association *www.usaboxing.org*

Canada Amateur Boxing Association *www.boxing.ca*

Golden Gloves Association *www.goldengloves.com*

Police Athletic League *www.nationalpal.org*

Boxing Resource Center *www.boxingresource.com*

Supportive Material

Equipment and Apparel Resources

Amber Sporting Goods
18075 West Little York
Katy, TX 77449
877-859-9565
www.ambersports.com

Balazs Boxing, Inc.
1129 W. Walnut Street
Allentown, PA 18102
888-466-6765
www.balazsboxing.com

Boxing Resource Center
P.O. Box 694
Brentwood, TN 37027-0694
www.BoxingResource.com

Cansco International, Inc.
8568 Bethany Lane
Cincinnati, OH 45255
513-474-6342
www.CanscoSportingGoods.com

Cleto Reyes Boxing
Wagner 289 Col. Vallego
Mexico D.F. 07870
(52) 5537-2851
www.cletoreyes.com.mx

Elite
6 Crighton Place
Leith Walk
Edinburgh EH7 4NZ
Scotland, UK
www.elite-sports.co.uk

Everlast Sports Mfg. Co.
750 East 132nd Street
Bronx, NY 10454
800-221-8777
www.everlast.com

Grant Boxing Goods
234 5th Ave.
New York, NY 10001
877-472-6801
www.grantboxing.com

Ringside, Inc.
9650 Dice Lane
Lenexa, KS 66215
877-426-9464
www.ringside.com

Title Boxing
P.O. Box 409
Shawnee Mission, KS 66201
800-999-1213
www.titleboxing.com

TKO
P.O. Box 0035 Ellicott Station
Buffalo, NY 14205
800-267-4886
www.tkogear.com

Tuf-Wear
202 S. Birch Street
Kimball, NE 69145
800-404-0780
www.tufwear.com

Movies About Boxing

The following list of movies includes mainstream and independently produced films in which boxing plays a significant role, or features a character who is a boxer. Some of these productions are compilations of professional fights and interviews with professional boxers. Though most of the older films cannot be rented at local rental stores, you can still find some played on cable television or rent them through mail-order rental companies.

Movies are listed in alphabetical order within production year. The year of production, director(s), country of production, and running time are also listed, where available.

I Spy (2002, Betty Thomas, USA, 96 mins.)
Undisputed (2002, Walter Hill, USA, 94 mins.)
Ali (2001, Michael Mann, USA, 156 mins.)
Carmen the Champion (2001, Lee Stanley, USA, 90 mins.)
Muhammad Ali: The Greatest/Ali & The Fighter (2001, USA, 60 mins.)
Muhammad Ali: In His Own Words/Skills, Brains, & Guts (2001, USA, 130 mins.)
Muhammad Ali: Through the Eyes of the World (2001, Phil Grabsky, USA, 104 mins.)
Out Kold (2001, Detdrich McClure, USA, 82 mins.)
Billy Elliot (2000, Stephen Daldry, UK, 110 mins.)
Boxing's Been Good to Me (2000, Temple Brown, USA, 15 mins.)
Girlfight (2000, Karyn Kusama, USA, 111 mins.)
Kings of the Ring (2000, Bud Greenspan, USA)
Knockout (2000, Lorenzo Doumani, USA, 100 mins.)
Muhammad Ali: King of the World (2000, John Secret Young, USA)
The Opponent (2000, Eugene Jarecki, USA, 90 mins.)
Price of Glory (2000, Carlos Avila, USA, 118 mins.)
Shiner (2000, John Irvin, Great Britain, 98 mins.)
Snatch (2000, Guy Ritchie, USA, 103 mins.)
Straight Right (2000, P. David Ebersole, USA, 90 mins.)
Bao (1999, William D. Mar/Johnny Joo, USA, 74 mins.)
The Hurricane (1999, Norman Jewison, USA, 146 mins.)
Love's Song (1999, Louis Gossett, Jr., USA, 120 mins.)
Muhammad Ali: The Greatest Collection (1999, 289 mins.)
On the Ropes (1999, Nanette Burstein/Brett Morgen, USA, 90 mins.)
Play it to the Bone (1999, USA, Ron Shelton, 125 mins.)
Rocky Marciano (1999, Charles Winkler, USA, 99 mins.)
Shadow Boxers (1999, Katya Bankowsky, USA, 72 mins.)
Southpaw: The Francis Barrett Story (1999, Liam McGrath, Ireland, 76 mins.)
Body and Soul (1998, Sam Kass, USA, 95 mins.)
Legionnaire (1998, Peter MacDonald, USA, 98 mins.)

Supportive Material

Like It Is (1998, Paul Oremland, Great Britian, 95 mins.)
Love Is the Devil (1998, John Maybury, Great Britain, 88 mins.)
Mob Queen (1998, Jon Carnoy, USA, 87 mins.)
Snake Eyes (1998, Brian DePalma, USA, 98 mins.)
TwentyFourSeven (1998, Shane Meadows, Great Britain, 96 mins.)
The Boxer (1997, Jim Sheridan, USA/Ireland, 113 mins.)
Don King: Only in America (1997, John Herzfeld, USA, 112 mins.)
The Kid (1997, John Hamilton, USA, 89 mins.)
Muhammad Ali: The Whole Story (1997, USA, documentary series Vols. 1-6)
When We Were Kings (1997, Leon Cast, USA, 90 mins.)
The Great White Hype (1996, Reginald Hudlin, USA, 91 mins.)
Journey of the African-American Athlete (1996, William Rhoden, USA, 119 mins.)
Le Montreur De Boxe (1996, Dominique Ladoge, France, 100 mins.)
Les Miserables (1995, Claude Lelouch, France, 175 mins.)
Low (1995, Lise Raven, USA, 95 mins.)
Rude (1995, Clement Vigo, Canada, 89 mins.)
Tokyo Fist (1995, Shinya Tsukamoto, Japan, 85 mins.)
Boxer Rebellion (1994, Celia Cotelo, USA, 73 mins.)
Fallen Champ: The Untold Story of Mike Tyson (1993, Barbara Kopple, USA)
Forced to Kill (1993, Russell Solberg, USA, 93 mins.)
Boxing: The Best of the 1980s, Vols. 1 & 2 (1992, USA, 50/52 mins.)
Boxing Bloopers & KOs (1992, USA, 30 mins.)
Diggstown (1992, Michael Ritchie, USA, 98 mins.)
Gladiator (1992, Rowdy Herrington, USA, 101 mins.)
Muhammad Ali: Fighter of the Century (1992, Steve Lott, USA, 73 mins.)
Night and the City (1992, Irwin Winkler, USA, 104 mins.)
Ballad of the Sad Cafe (1991, Simon Callow, USA/Great Britian, 100 mins.)
Blonde Fist (1991, Frank C. Clarke, UK, 100 mins.)
Dreams of Glory: A Boxer's Story (1991, Lawrence Lau, Hong Kong)
Muhammad Ali: The Greatest (1991, documentary, USA, 109 mins.)
The Big Bang (1990, James Toback, USA, 81 mins.)
The Big Man (1990, David Leland, UK, 93 mins.)
Rocky V (1990, John Avildsen, USA, 105 mins.)
Boxing's Best: Muhammad Ali (1989, USA, 50 mins.)
Champions Forever (1989, Dimitri Logothetis, USA, 120 mins.)
Triumph of the Spirit (1989, Robert M. Young, USA, 115 mins.)
Homeboy (1988, Michael Seresin, USA, 116 mins.)
Broken Noses (1987, Bruce Weber, USA, 75 mins.)
Streets of Gold (1986, Joe Roth, USA, 95 mins.)
Detective (1985, Jean-Luc Godard, France, 95 mins.)
Joe Louis—For All Time (1985, Peter Tatum, USA, 89 mins.)
Rocky IV (1985, Sylvester Stallone, USA, 91 mins.)
Deadly Duo (1983, Yu Wan Chuen, Hong Kong)
Dempsey (1983, Gus Trikonis, USA, 110 mins.)
Honeyboy (1982, John Berry, USA, 100 mins.)

Legends of the Ring (1982 - 1989, documentary series)
Penitentiary II (1982, Jamaa Fanaka, USA, 103 mins.)
Rocky III (1982, Sylvester Stallone, USA, 100 mins.)
Body and Soul (1981, George Bowers, USA, 100 mins.)
Goldie and the Boxer Go To Hollywood (1981, David Miller, USA, 100 mins.)
Raging Bull (1980, Martin Scorsese, USA, 127 mins.)
The Champ (1979, Franco Zeffirelli, USA, remake, 117 mins.)
Goldie and the Boxer (1979, David Miller, USA, 100 mins.)
The Main Event (1979, Howard Zieff, USA, 105 mins.)
Penitentiary (1979, Jamaa Fanaka, USA, 99 mins.)
The Prize Fighter (1979, Michael Preece, USA, 99 mins.)
Rocky II (1979, Sylvester Stallone, USA, 120 mins.)
Movie Movie (1978, Stanley Donen, USA, 115 mins.)
The Boxer (1977, Shuji Terayama, Japan, 95 mins.)
The Greatest (1977, Tom Gries and Monte Hellman, USA, 102 mins.)
America in Black & White, Pugs 'N Pols (1976, Scott Jacobs, USA, 40 mins.)
Rocky (1976, John G. Avildsen, USA, 119 mins.)
Ali the Man: Ali the Fighter (1975, William Greaves, USA, 142 mins.)
Legends of the Ring: Muhammad Ali (1975, USA, 87 mins.)
The Fighters (1974, William Greaves, USA, 114 mins.)
Muhammad Ali, The Greatest (1974, William Klein, France, 120 mins.)
Boxing's Best: Sugar Ray Robinson (1972, USA, documentary, 60 mins.)
Fat City (1972, John Huston, USA, 100 mins.)
Ripped Off (1971, Franco Prosperi, Italy, 80 mins.)
The Great White Hope (1970, Martin Ritt, USA, 102 mins.)
Jack Johnson, The Big Fights (1970, William Cayton, USA, 88 mins.)
Muhammad Ali a.k.a. Cassius Clay (1970, Jim Jacobs, USA, 79 mins.)
The Happiest Millionaire (1967, Norman Tokar, USA, 164 mins.)
Boxer and Death (1963, Peter Solan, Czechoslavakia, 120 mins.)
Kid Galahad (1962, Phil Karlson, USA, 95 mins.)
Requiem for a Heavyweight (1962, Ralph Nelson, USA, 95 mins.)
Rocco and His Brothers (1960, Luchino Visconti, Italy, 134 mins.)
Fight for the Title (1957, Eric Kenton, USA, 30 mins.)
Monkey on My Back (1957, André De Toth, USA, 94 mins.)
The Harder They Fall (1956, Mark Robson, USA, 109 mins.)
Requiem for a Heavyweight (1956, Ralph Nelson, USA, 89 mins.)
Somebody Up There Likes Me (1956, Robert Wise, USA, 113 mins.)
Killer's Kiss (1955, Stanley Kubrick, USA, 67 mins.)
On the Waterfront (1954, Elia Kazan, USA, 108 mins.)
The Joe Louis Story (1953, Robert Gordon, USA, 88 mins.)
Kid Monk Baroni (1952, Harold Schuster, USA, 80 mins.)
The Quiet Man (1952, John Ford, USA, 153 mins.)
The Ring (1952, Kurt Neumann, USA, 79 mins.)
Abbott and Costello Meet the Invisible Man (1951, Charles Lamont, USA, 82 mins.)
The Fighter (1951, Herbert Kline, USA, 78 mins.)

Supportive Material

Champion (1949, Mark Robson, USA, 99 mins.)
The Set Up (1949, Robert Wise, USA, 72 mins.)
In This Corner (1948, Charles Riesner, USA, 62 mins.)
Body and Soul (1947, Robert Rossen, USA, 104 mins.)
Kid from Brooklyn (1946, Norman Z. McLeod, USA, 113 mins.)
Footlight Serenade (1942, Gregory Ratoff, USA, 81 mins.)
Gentleman Jim (1942, Raoul Walsh, USA, 104 mins.)
Here Comes Mr. Jordan (1941, Alexander Hall, USA, 94 mins.)
The Pittsburg Kid (1941, Jack Townley, USA, 76 min.)
City for Conquest (1940, Anatole Litvak, USA, 101 mins.)
Golden Boy (1939, Rouben Manoulian, USA, 99 mins.)
They Made Me a Criminal (1939, Busby Berkeley, USA, 92 mins.)
Join the Marines (1937, Ralph Staub, USA, 70 mins.)
Spirit of Youth (1937, Harry Fraser, USA, 70 mins.)
When's Your Birthday? (1937, Harry Beaumont, USA, 76 mins.)
The Milky Way (1936, Leo McCarey, USA, 89 mins.)
Swing to the Left (1936, Jacques Tati, France, short)
Belle of the Nineties (1934, Leo McCarey, USA, 73 mins.)
The Big Chance (1933, Albert Herman, USA, 60 mins.)
The Prizefighter and the Lady (1933, W.S. Van Dyke, USA, 102 mins.)
Night After Night (1932, Archie Mayo, USA, 70 mins.)
Winner Take All (1932, Roy Del Ruth, USA, 66 mins.)
The Champ (1931, King Vidor, USA, 87 mins.)
The Tip Off (1931, Albert S. Rogell, USA, 71 mins.)
Be Yourself (1930, Thorton Freeland, USA, 77 mins.)
Boxing Gloves (1929, Robert McGowan, USA)
Dress Parade (1927, Donald Crisp, USA, 72 mins.)
The Ring (1927, Alfred Hitchcock, Great Britain, 82 mins., silent)
Battling Butler (1926, Buster Keaton, USA, 78 mins., silent with music)
One Punch O'Day (1926, Harry J. Brown, USA, 60 mins.)
Twinkletoes (1926, Charles Babin, USA, 78 mins., silent with music)
The Wildcat (1926, Harry L. Fraser, USA, 52 mins., silent)
His People (1925, Edward Sloman, USA, 91 mins., silent)
Battling Fool (1924, W.S. Van Dyke, USA, 56 mins., silent with music track)
Boxing: An Analysis of Motion (1919, USA, documentary, silent)

Glossary of Boxing Terms

alphabet soup: slang used to describe the large number of organizations that host championships for professional boxers; specifically refers to the official-sounding acronyms of these organizations and to the difficulty of keeping track of them.

amateur boxing: boxing which is done without monetary compensation and under the guidance of a National Governing Body (NGB). The International Amateur Boxing Association (AIBA) governs international competition between NGBs.

angles: see "taking angles"

anterior: front of the body

apron: the part of the ring floor that extends between the outside of the ropes and the edge of the platform. Aprons are typically 24" wide to accommodate personnel who work on the boxer between rounds, and to prevent boxers from slipping out of the ring.

ball of foot: the widest part of the foot, just beneath the toes

backpedal: retreating (quickly) backwards while facing the opponent

baseball: slang used to describe an overhand cross that is thrown over the opponent's guard—the action resembles the way one would throw a baseball.

be first: to hit or feint the opponent in order to initiate action

bell: klaxon, whistle, or other device that signals the beginning and end of a round or bout

beltline: invisible line around the torso of the boxer, extending from the top of each hip bone and through the navel. Trunks are worn at the beltline to mark the legal and illegal regions of the body.

blind corner/area: area of the ring in which the majority of judges do not have a good view of the punches being thrown.

block: deflection of a punch with the gloves, arms, elbows, or shoulders

blow: a punch (see also, "scoring blow")

bobbing: ducking down and up to evade punches

body shot/punch: blow to the body of an opponent

box: the act of boxing; also the command given by the referee to proceed boxing after the "stop" command has been issued

boxer: one who boxes in a skilled manner

boxing shoes: shoes that feature flat soles to promote movement in the ring. Most boxing shoes (or "boots") lace to the ankle or mid-calf.

Glossary

boxing zone: space in which the boxers are within striking distance of each other

break: release of an opponent when clinched/holding; also a command given by the amateur referee which requires the boxers to let go and take one step away from their opponent before they continue boxing

breast protector: material used to cover the chest of a female boxer, may be constructed from dense foam, thin plastic, cotton, or nylon

butt: see "head butt"

button: the point of the chin

butterfly strips: thin adhesive strips used to close a cut

card: term used to refer to the schedule of a boxing show; comprised of an "undercard" and "main event"

catch: similar to a parry, the catch is made with the open glove to "catch" the knuckles of the opponent's glove

champ: nickname for someone who is a champion; some "champs" are champions as a result of their character, and others are considered "champs" due to winning a championship bout

chump: an opponent who, in professional boxing, is known to lose easily (and is paid precisely to do so)

clinch: holding with straight arms, or locking arms with the opponent. Punches are not exchanged during a clinch.

college boxing: novice amateur boxing conducted through colleges/universities. In the U.S. college boxing is sanctioned under the National Collegiate Boxing Association (NCBA), a group member of USA Boxing, Inc.

commission: professional organization which oversees boxing in a region, or for a particular organization

computerized scoring: system in which judges record every scoring blow observed via a keypad linked to a computer which calculates majority-witnessed scoring blows, reflecting an overall total score

cornerman: one who works a boxer's corner (usually the boxer's coach/trainer)

counterpunch: a punch thrown in reaction to the opponent's punch

cross: slang for strong-side punch (the right hand for a right-hander)

croucher: boxer who bends the torso and legs in order to keep low and lead with the head

cut man: the person who is responsible for closing cuts, minimizing bleeding, and reducing swelling during professional fights (paid by the boxer, manager, or promoter, depending on the contract)

counted out: when a boxer is downed, the referee commences counting to ten. If the boxer is still hurt (down) by the count of 10, the referee will declare the bout over.
crunch: variation on the traditional sit-up in which the abdominal muscles are contracted only enough to lift the shoulders off the floor
distance: the space between you and your opponent in which you can make contact with a punch
double-end bag: a round practice bag, attached to the ceiling and floor with elastic cords, that moves rapidly when punched; used to improve skill building, coordination, agility, and stamina
double jab: throwing two jabs in rapid succession
down the pipe: slang for a punch that is thrown straight; "the pipe" is the imaginary line between your shoulder and your opponent
downstairs: slang for the contact zone of the opponent's body
drawing: a strategic move in which the boxer leaves an opening purposefully, in an attempt to "draw" the opponent into leading with a specific blow that can then be quickly countered
drop: to knock down an opponent
duck: defensive move in which the legs are bent so the opponent's punches miss overhead
dukes: slang for fists
dynamic warmup exercises: range-of-motion and joint rotation exercises that prepare the body for interval, plyometric, and boxing workouts
eight-count: see "standing eight-count"
elbowing: a foul in which the elbow strikes the opponent
elimination fighting: a single-elimination contest in which winners of contests progress through the course of a night or series of nights in order to be crowned the winner. Elimination fighters are usually paid only if they win the entire event.
enswell: metal device (cooled in ice or ice water) used to reduce swelling on the face during the rest intervals of a bout or fight
extreme fighting: no-holds-barred fighting, outlawed in many parts of the United States and around the world
feint: an offensive technique in which the boxer gestures as if he/she is going to throw a punch, so as to provoke an offensive or defensive counter from the opponent.
five-punch: the lead-side uppercut (left hand, if right-handed)
focus mitts: a.k.a punch pads; flat pads worn on the hands of the coach as targets for a boxer to practice movement and combinations.

Glossary

footwork: movement of the feet and legs
foul: infraction of a rule
four-punch: the strong-side upper cut (right hand, if right handed)
gauze: roll of cotton weave used by professionals to wrap hands for competition
glass jaw: term used to describe a boxer who goes down easily after being hit in the jaw/head
gloves: worn on the hands to protect while training or competing. Gloves vary by weight, closure, color, and thumb attachment.
go the distance: a bout that lasts the scheduled number of rounds
Golden Gloves: group member under USA Boxing, Inc.
grease: slang for lubricant (such as petroleum jelly) used on the face or body to minimize the effectiveness of an opponent's blows
groin protector: padding that covers the groin area of a boxer, may be composed of dense foam, protective cup, and/or padded leather. Typical designs wrap-around the beltline, and are tied in the back.
half-step back: an evasive movement of the legs and torso in which the back foot moves straight backwards while the front foot remains in place. From this position the boxer can quickly explode forward into a boxing stance, using the back foot as leverage.
handwraps: bands of fabric (usually 2" x 180") used to protect the hands under the gloves; may be made of cotton, Velpeau or gauze. Handwraps are worn in practice and competition.
haymaker: a wild punch thrown (usually in desperation) in a effort to knock out an opponent
head butt: using the head to impact the opponent's head; this is a dangerous foul since it can easily cut the face and/or damage the eye
headgear: protective "helmet" worn in amateur bouts and/or in practice, made of soft, dense material such as foam, covered with leather or soft plastic
heavy hands: term used to describe a boxer who throws a lot of hard (knockout-type) punches
heavybag: oblong bag weighing 70 lbs.+ used to practice punching; some bags are hung horizontally to facilitate throwing uppercuts
holding: foul that consists of grabbing the opponent at the arms, gloves, waist, or behind the head
hook: (also known as #3 punch) a swinging punch thrown to either the head or the body of the opponent
in the pocket: slang for elbows that are close to the body

infighting: boxing within close range of the opponent
interval: pre-set duration for an exercise or rest
interval running: sets of sprints used in a running program
jab: (also known as #1 punch) a straight punch thrown with the lead hand (the left hand for right-handers); the most often used punch
kayo: knockout, results in the termination of a professional fight
kidney punch: illegal punch that lands on the lower back
KO: knockout; results in the termination of a professional fight
knockdown: when a boxer touches the floor as the result of a blow
knockout: situation in which a boxer touches the floor as the result of a blow, and cannot continue to box by the referee's count
low blow: an illegal blow that contacts the boxer below the belt line
manager: person who schedules professional fights for a pugilist
machine gunning: slang used to describe throwing punches (usually upper cuts) in rapid succession
main event: portion of a boxing card considered the main attraction, comprised of one or two bouts, typically scheduled as the finale.
majority decision: a decision in which most of the judges voted for the same winner
majority draw: a decision in which the majority of the judges voted that the contest was a tie
making weight: the process of adjusting the body's composition in order to lose or gain weight so as to qualify for a specific weight class
matchmaking: process of pairing up opponents for competition
maze ball: a small, pear-shaped bag (usually filled with sand) hung to practice head and body movements such as slipping/sliding and ducking, and integrating those movements with shadow punches
mercy rule: see "outscore rule"
mismatch: situation in which boxers are not of similar skill levels, where one is clearly better than the other
mouse: swelling (hematoma) on the forehead or under the eye as the result of a punch, head butt, elbow, etc.
mouthpiece: protective insert for the mouth, used to protect teeth and jaw, made of rubber or plastic
neutral corner: one of two corners in the ring that have been designated as neutral not used by the boxers during the rest interval
Olympic-style boxing: see "amateur boxing"
one-punch: the jab
open side: dominant side of a boxer (the right side if a right-handed)

Glossary

out: when a boxer is dazed (a.k.a. "out on his/her feet") or is completely non-responsive

outbox: to skillfully box decidedly better than the other boxer

outscore rule: allows for the termination of a bout in computerized scoring if one boxer outscores the other by a predetermined amount

out point: winning a decision on points

overhand cross: a cross that is thrown over the opponent's guard

PAL: Police Athletic League. A group member under USA Boxing.

paper scoring: traditional scoring in which judges record their scores on paper scorecards after the completion of each round of the bout

parry: deflection of opponent's punch by redirecting the movement with the open glove

peanut: slang for head

posterior: back of the body

power punch: slang for the cross

prizefighter: professional boxer

professional boxing: boxing/fighting in which participants are paid with money or other prizes, including elimination boxing contests

promoter: person who coordinates professional cards and pays participants

pugilist: one who combats with the fists

punch pads: see "focus mitts"

purse: slang for the payment that a professional boxer receives for performing on a boxing card

R.I.C.E.: system used to treat minor injuries: rest, ice, compression, elevation

rabbit punch: an illegal blow to the back of the neck

reach: the distance from the tip of the fingertips of one hand, across the back, to the fingers of the other hand

recovery: rest interval allowed between exercises, or the time allowed between workouts

rest bell: the bell that signifies the beginning of the rest interval

retirement: voluntary stopping of a bout via the coach/trainer, or the boxer, who announces to the referee that the bout will not continue

right cross: the straight right-handed punch of a right-handed boxer (also known as #2, power punch)

ring: square roped area, with four padded corners, and a padded floor covered by canvas or vinyl, in which boxing competitions occurs

ring rust: slang for feeling lathargic and/or awkward after an extended break from competition

road work: slang for running/jogging

rolling: an evasive move in which the head and/or body is moved along in the same direction of the opponent's punches

RSC: referee stops contest, a term used in amateur boxing in which the referee terminates the bout

scoring blow: a blow that lands in the target area of the opponent, has not been picked, parried, or blocked by the opponent, was thrown with the weight of the shoulder and/or body, made contact with the knuckle part of the glove, and was thrown without committing a foul

scorecard: paper slip on which judges record their scores for each round, the total score for the bout, and indicate their chosen winner

second: the person in the corner who cares for the boxer during a bout

second skin: product used to promote the healing of a cut by providing a clear, moist coating over the wound

seconds out: the auditory warning for all coaches and assistants to leave the ring and apron for the start of the next round

shiner: slang for a black eye

side-step: see "taking angles"

Silver Gloves: a group member of USA Boxing, Inc.

slap: an illegal hit using the palm, rather than the knuckle, of the glove. Slaps usually make a loud noise.

slide: an evasive move in which the legs and waist bend over the plane of the lead thigh to allow the oncoming punch to move past the ear

slip: an evasive move in which the legs and waist bend over the plane of the strong thigh to allow the oncoming punch to move past the ear; term also refers to a situation in which a boxer accidentally touches the ring canvas as a result of tripping, getting tangled in the opponent's feet, or falling due to moisture on the canvas

slug fest: a bout in which both boxers are heavy-handed, generally trying to knock each other out

slugger: someone who likes to fight, or who attempts to knock out opponents with big punches, rather than by boxing

smothering punches: moving too close to the target so that full extension of the punches cannot be achieved

southpaw: slang for a left-handed boxer

speedbag: a pear-shaped, air-filled bag often used in boxing workouts, used for building coordination and stamina in the shoulders

Glossary

split decision: a.k.a. majority decision, decision in which all judges do not unanimously agree on the winner

sprints: see "interval running"

square circle: slang for boxing ring

square heels: slang used to describe someone who never seems to get knocked down, despite the punches received

standing-eight count: a count given to a boxer who is still standing, but who appears to be possibly hurt or overmatched. After the count of eight, the referee decides whether or not the bout can continue.

stiff jab: a jab that is thrown with directed power while advancing toward the opponent, with the intention of forcing the opponent to move backwards

stop: a command given by a referee for boxers to stop the action and look to the referee for instructions or commands. If the referee gives the command to stop, he/she must give the command to "box" in order for action to resume in amateur boxing.

stopped: a contest terminated by retirement or referee's command

strong side: a boxer's power side (the right side on a right-handed boxer)

super-set: weight-lifting term that describes the technique of alternating between two exercises until the sets for each exercise are completed.

Swiss ball: large air-filled plastic ball used for various exercises, such as push-ups and abdominal exercises

taking angles: moving to the side of the opponent so that you are in position to contact him/her while simultaneously moving out of range of the opponent's punches

tale of the tape: phrase used to describe the physical matchup of boxers in competition, referencing specifically their age, weight, height, reach, and record

technical knockout: a situation in professional boxing in which the referee stops the fight due to the belief that one boxer is hurt and cannot continue safely

telegraphing the punch: indicating to your opponent what you are about to do (for example, dropping the hand, or cocking the shoulder just before you throw a punch)

tempo: the rhythm of a round or bout

ten-point must system: system in which boxing judges award 10 points to the winner of each round, and fewer points to the loser

TKO: see "technical knockout"

tied up: slang for a situation in which both boxers are clinched, or where one is intentionally holding the other to prevent being hit
toe-to-toe: standing directly in front of an opponent to trade blows
Toughman Contest: elimination fight tournament in which the winner takes all of the prize money or awards
three-punch: the hook
timing: ability to coordinate contact at the moment an opening occurs
twenty-point must system: system in which boxing judges award 20 points to the winner of each round, and fewer points to the loser
two-punch: the straight cross (thrown with the dominant hand)
u-dip: ducking while simultaneously moving to the right and/or left
unanimous decision: when all judges vote for the same winner of a bout
undercard: portion of a boxing show that is not considered part of the main event
unorthodox: slang for a boxer who does not box in a traditional manner; used to describe a left-handed boxer
uppercut: a punch thrown in an upward manner, with the palm facing the thrower (also known as #4 or #5 punch)
upstairs: slang for the contact zone of the head
v-step: see "taking angles"
v-step on approach: the action of approaching your opponent at an angle, rather than engaging directly in front of him or her
Velpeau: elastic-like cotton webbing used for wrapping hands; amateur boxers are allowed 2.5 meters of material on each hand
weak side: a boxer's lead side (the left side on a right-handed boxer)
weaving: evasive move in which the boxer bends the legs and torso repeatedly down, to the right, and to the left to avoid being hit
Western-style boxing: traditional boxing style; differentiated from "Eastern" martial arts
work bell: the bell that signifies the interval in which to exercise during a workout; typically two to three minutes in duration

Bibliography

Campbell, C., I. Postma, et al., Eds. (1998). *USA Boxing: Official rules 1998-1999*. Colorado Springs, United States Amateur Boxing, Inc.

Degtiariov, I. P. (Ed.) (1979.) *Boxeo: Manual para los institutos de cultura física*. Moscow, Editorial Raduga.

Early, G. (1994). *The culture of bruising: Essays on prizefighting, literature, and modern American culture*. Hopewell, N.J., Ecco Press.

Gorn, E. (1986). *The manly art: Bare-knuckle prize fighting in America*. Ithaca, Cornell University Press.

Guttmann, A. (1991). *Women's sports: A history*. New York, Columbia.

Hare, N. (1971). "A study of the black fighter." *The Black Scholar* November: 2-8.

Halbert, C. (1997). "Tough enough and woman enough: Stereotypes, discrimination, and impression management among women professional boxers," *Journal of Sport and Social Issues*, Vol. 21, No. 1, pp. 7-36.

Hargreaves, J. (1996). "Bruising Peg to boxerobics: Gendered boxing—images and meanings". *Boxer: An anthology of writings on boxing and visual culture*. D. Chandler, J. Gill, T. Guha and G. Tawadros. Cambridge, MIT Press: 121-131.

Holcomb, W., Kleiner, D., and Chu, D. (1998). "Plyometrics: Considerations for safe and effective training." *Strength and Conditioning*, June 1998: 36-39.

Jordan, B. M., E. Matser, et al. (1996). "Sparring and cognitive function in professional boxers." *The Physician and Sportsmedicine* 24(5): 87-98.

Kotz, C. (1998). *Boxing for everyone: How to get fit and have fun with boxing*. Seattle, AmandaLore Publishing.

Lee, B. (1975). *Tao of Jeet Kune Do*. Santa Clarita, CA, Ohara Publications.

Oates, J. C. (1987). *On Boxing*. New York, Doubleday.

Priest, R., A. Vitters, et al. (1978). "Coeducation at West Point." *Armed Forces and Society* 4: 589-606.

Sammons, J. (1988). *Beyond the ring: The role of boxing in American society*. Urbana, University of Illinois Press.

Sugden, J. (1987). "The exploitation of disadvantage: The occupational sub-culture of the boxer." *The Sociological Review Monograph* 33: 187-209.

unknown (1905). "The model maid will help her health by boxing." *Evening World*. New York.

Wacquant, L. (1992). "The social logic of boxing in black Chicago: Toward a sociology of pugilism." *Sociology of Sport Journal* 9: 221-54.

Weinberg, S. K. and H. Arond (1952). "The occupational culture of the boxer." *American Journal of Sociology* 52: 460-69.

Index

AIBA 131, 190, 195, 221
abdominal exercises 77-81
abdominal muscles 40, 77, 86
absorb (see "block")
aerobics 60-62, 210
amateur boxing 11, 195, 202, 220-221
   compared to professional 190-194, 203
   competition 108-114, 148, 174-186
   fouls and referee signals 30, 130-133
   injury 87, 203-204, 206-208
   women 199-202
angles
   on approach 45-46, 142-143
   on defense 143-144
   while engaged 23, 45-46, 142-144
ankle weights 66
Arond, H. 196-198, 237
back exercises 82-83, 86
backpedal 53, 154
ball of the foot 21, 32, 37
bananas 124
bicycle 78-81
black eye 208
bleach 59
blind zone 180-182
blinding jab 145-146
block 39-40, 110-111
bobbing 46, 141
body
   scoring zone 27, 146-147
   drawing to the 44-45
   body types 121, 123
boxaerobics 202, 210
boxer (see "boxing styles")
boxing styles
   boxer 171-172
   croucher 170
   left-handed opponent 167-168
   shorter opponent 165-166
   slugger 172-173
   taller opponent 166-167
   wild fighter 169-170
boxing zone 35-36, 116, 136-137, 142-143
break 110, 130, 140, 186
breast protectors 119, 187

burnout drill 54, 61
Canada 192, 200, 221
calisthenics 66
canvas 23, 183-184
cardiovascular fitness 60, 63, 67-71, 91
care of boxing equipment 59
catch (see "parry")
chin 22-23, 27, 32-34, 38-41, 70, 138
classism 197-198
clinching 140, 148, 170
competition, what to expect
   amateur boxing 185-186
   professional boxing 187-188
computerized scoring 152, 176-179, 195
cornerman 206
covering 47, 111, 140, 144, 147, 165, 171, 173
cross 32-35, 39, 145, 150
croucher (see "boxing styles")
crunch 78-81
cutting off the ring 184
dehydration 123-125
distance running 68-70
double-end bag 23, 54-55
draw 174
drawing 44-45
dynamic warmup 70-71, 96
Early, Gerald 237
electronic scoring (see "computerized")
evasive tactics 45, 140-141
executive boxing 202, 210
fatigue, signs of 147-148
feint 38, 44-46
female boxers (see "women")
first aid 207
fitness boxing 202-203, 210, 220
food 123-125, 208
forced openings 147
fouls 131-133
"great white hope" 197-198
groin protector 119, 185, 187
guarding 39, 45, 109-113, 137, 147
Guttmann, Alan 237
half-step back 41-43, 141
handwraps 59, 87, 120, 126-129
Hare, Nathan 196-198, 237

Index

Hargreaves, J 202, 237
head trauma 203-204, 209
headgear 59, 117, 153, 185, 191-193, 209
heavy bag 54, 148
HIV 59
infighting 36, 41, 46, 140-141, 179
interval training 63, 68-71
jump rope 61, 63-65
Kotz, Cappy 13, 237
ladders 54
lazy jab 26, 28, 39, 145
Lee, Bruce 149, 237
left-hander (see "boxing styles")
maze ball 23, 54, 56
medicine ball 97-101
milk 124-125, 208
mirror work 19, 52
mouthpiece 118-119, 153, 185-187
muscle memory 16, 156
neck 73, 85, 88, 204
novice (see "boxing styles")
Oates, Joyce Carol 237
on guard position 22, 24-27
paper scoring (see "scoring")
pivot 23-24
plyometrics 95-106
potassium 124
power, punching with 148
power drill 54
power punch (see "cross")
Priest, R. 237
professional boxing (see "amateur")
punch pads (see "focus mitts")
R.I.C.E. 207
racism 195-198
recovery time/interval 67, 69-70, 121
referee signals 131-133
resistance training 66, 84-106
rest (see "recovery")
ring generalship 110, 176, 178, 186
ring specifications 183-184
roadwork (see "distance running")
rolling 19, 34, 141
rope duck 53, 138
rubber- band punches 57
Sammons, J 237
scoring 108-110, 174-179
second impact syndrome 204

shoulder push 130
side step 45-46
skipping rope (see "jumping rope")
slide (see "slip)
slap 108, 169
slugger (see "boxing styles")
slip 34-36
slip bag (see "maze ball")
sparring
  directed 20, 153, 155
  free-form 20, 153, 156-157
  one-step 20, 153-154
  partners 57-58, 116, 157
  two-step 20, 153-155
  with a novice 158-160
  with better boxers 161
speed bag 54-56
splitter 145
sprints (see "interval running")
standing eight count 147, 186, 191, 193
stretching 66-68, 71-77
Sugden, J. 197-198, 237
superstitions 208
target zones, aerobic activity 62
target zones, striking 26-27, 146-147
Total Resistance Training Program 91-94
USAB 110-111, 131-133, 200, 221
u-dip 53, 138, 141, 144
upper jab 55, 57, 145
Vitters, A 237
Wacquant, Loic 197-198, 237
warming up 52, 58, 62-63, 66-69, 70-72
weaving 141
weight classes 121-123
weight loss 68, 121, 123-125
weighted punches 57
wild fighter (see "boxing styles")
Weinberg, S 237
women 119, 157, 190, 199-202
wrist 22, 87, 90, 92